# THE POWER OF SERVICE

## SERVICE THROUGH THE EYES OF CUSTOMERS

# *Acknowledgements*

## *A Big 'Thank-you' to:*

CanNor for their support of the Service Project at the Whitehorse Chamber of Commerce

Yukon Entrepreneurship Centre—Sponsor

Whitehorse Chamber of Commerce for its Collaboration & Support

Danielle Hession -- Front Cover Designer

Richard Hession -- For his Mentorship

Jocelyn Hession -- My Guru

Richard the Lion Heart—My Guide and Inspiration

and

To those Friends and Associates who gave me input, encouragement and support along the way.

# *Dedication*

*This book is dedicated to those People who have committed themselves happily to Serving Customers beyond their expectations, and to those who have inspired me and others to feel good about themselves, through their everyday actions and words.*

*J.E. Karp*



ISBN 978-0-9936547-0-1

cover design by Danielle Hession

Printed and bound in Whitehorse, Yukon
by Integraphics Ltd.
January 2014
For information contact,
www.whitehorsechamber.ca

# *Introduction*

## *Is there a secret to success coming from terrific Service?*

What is it that leads to success in one business, while others in the same industry struggle? This question is especially relevant today in a climate where it is not just difficult to do business, but there are unique challenges that make every competitive edge a "must do".

Through an engaging storyline, the Author of **The Power of Service** presents a number of key lessons that have significant relevance for businesses and organizations everywhere. These lessons can be applied to build sales and customer transactions as well as propel the value perception of your business. It will also teach all of us who work the benefits of providing service excellence and how to make it a reality.

Storytelling is one of the oldest forms of communication; and through the story of Josh and Monica the author, J.E. Karp, shows us what great service should look like! Josh and Monica's final "Presentation" synthesizes all of their experiences into a "how to" explanation of what customers want and how to give it to them.

The Service experiences and strategies in this book can help grow your career and your business and have the potential to enrich your life. Then there are the quotes at the beginning of some of the chapters, and the highlighted statements that add so much meaning to the book.

As the leader of a business organization and owner of a business, I have found this Book to be very helpful and to the point. In addition, its unique approach engages the reader from beginning to end. I highly recommend it.

***President--WCC***

## Table of Contents

# Chapter 1

## The Situation

***"Screw It. Let's Do it."***

***Richard Branson—Founder Virgin Group***

Joshua and Monica were about to embark upon an unexpected set of experiences that would transform their lives forever. If anyone had told Monica or Josh that a series of events related to customer service was about to change their lives, neither of them would have bet one cent on that prediction. In fact, customer service was the furthest thing from their minds.

Since the ninth grade, Josh and Monica had been good friends. Now at age thirty and thirty-one respectively, they both decided it was time to complete their Bachelor degrees in Business Administration. As they selected their courses, they saw one called 'Hospitality & Service—Winning Over the Customer'. Viewing this as an easy credit, they both decided to add this course to their syllabus.

You see, at the age of thirty, Josh had been feeling that he was getting nowhere in his professional life. All of the jobs he had worked at, since dropping out of university, were either part-time or term positions. He just couldn't seem to land a full-time job in his field of business administration or in anything remotely related to business. Josh had dropped out of university when he became a single Dad eight years earlier.

Joshua Victor Johnson was born in the United States. His parents had met in Cuba on separate vacations. Josh's Mother was of Scottish decent and his Father was African-American. When Josh was six years of age, his parents moved to Canada in hopes of finding better work and more opportunity. The whole family--Josh, his Sister Maureen and his Parents--loved to ski and so they chose the City of New Plateau as their Canadian home.

Josh looked very much like a mixture of both his parents, average height, about 5' 9" with a medium-build. He was fit and attractively toned and muscular, with a chocolate-brown complexion and quite good-looking, in a Terrence Howard kind of way. In fact, people would often say he resembled a young Terrence Howard. He had his Father's colouring and his Mother's beautiful eyes and smile.

Josh's son Bernard, affectionately called 'Bean', was eight years old. He lived with Josh and that in itself is a whole other story, which you will learn about later. For now, let's just say that Josh was a very committed Dad. No one was more precious to him than Bean. More than anything, Josh wanted to create a more promising future for Bean and himself.

Monica Janine Flowers, age thirty-one, was six months older than Josh. She had never been married although she had been involved in two unhappy relationships, the last of which left her especially miserable. She wanted to start fresh and just get on with her life as a single woman. She had suffered enough disappointment with relationships and was now determined to make her education and her future career the focal point of her life. However, she often fought sadness. Monica was trying very hard to create hope, the way that sometimes the sun peers through the clouds, as if it is struggling to turn an overcast day into a sunny one.

Like Josh, Monica had also run the gambit of part-time and term positions. After several conversations with Josh, they both decided it was worth taking out student loans to complete their education. Their goal was to complete their degrees in Business and to renew their outlook on life. They both knew that accomplishing these goals was critical if they had any chance of finding a good career. Although they both seemingly wanted a career which involved business, neither Josh nor Monica really knew exactly what it was they wanted professionally. They agreed that they would learn along the journey, as they discovered new worlds of information. About that fact, they both were very hopeful and optimistic.

Monica's parents moved to Canada during the Vietnam War. Monica was Canadian born. Like Josh, she came from a diverse multicultural background. In fact, this was the catalyst for their becoming friends in grade nine. Monica's Mother was of Italian decent and her Father had been born and raised in Boston, a robust Caucasian man who first met Monica's Mother when she was a personal trainer in a Boston fitness club, which he frequented. They had lived in New Plateau for almost twenty years.

Monica had a natural radiance. Her skin looked as if she had a perfect tan, no doubt the influence of her Italian heritage. Her hair was shoulder-length, thick and mahogany in colour, with some violet-red highlights. Her deep brown eyes were beautiful and her natural long eyelashes added to her alluring and striking appearance. Monica looked very much like her Mother, petite, about 5'3" and in excellent shape. When sad, her face could look quite ordinary but when she smiled, it was a completely new radiant face that lit up a room and made heads turn.

Registration day had finally arrived. Josh and Monica registered for their classes, including the Hospitality/Service class. They went out to dinner together to celebrate their renewed lives. They both felt nervous but were comforted by the fact that they were entering this new phase together. Their long-term friendship had served them both well in the past.

They talked about how great it would be if both of them could graduate. They discussed their course selection. They were excited and apprehensive but both were very focused. They felt certain they were going down the right road and that it would lead to a better future. In the meantime, they were determined to enjoy the process of education. The academic world was a welcome change for both of them and they talked about how they each wanted to learn and grow and how their attitudes had changed over the last eight years. They had always had the brains but now they also had the hunger.

Josh and Monica were taking four courses each. Both registered for Effective Advertising & Marketing plus an advanced Computer Science Course; then there was the Service and Hospitality Course. Monica also registered for a course called 'Women in Business' while Josh registered for Accounting III, a course that Monica had already completed.

# Chapter 2

## *Introducing Professor Sydney*

"Welcome to Hospitality & Service -Winning Over the Customer," bellowed Professor Sydney.

Josh & Monica looked around the classroom and were surprised at the number of students who had signed up for this course. Maybe they too were looking for an easy credit.

The Professor continued, "If you are looking for an easy credit, you have come to the wrong place."

Josh and Monica glanced at each other with an embarrassed smile, as if to say "Oh-oh".

"However," stated the Professor, "If you want to work in a business or government department which caters to the public, or if you have a dream of owning your own business, then I will tell you this: if you do not understand the importance of service or if you do not care to know the importance of outstanding service, and, if you do not wish to work diligently to learn what all that is, then now would be a good time for you to leave this room. However, If you do want to learn how splendid service and hospitality can change your life and the lives of others, then stick around and prepare yourself to learn and be the better for it. That is the power of outstanding service."

And there it was...Josh and Monica felt surprisingly motivated and inspired. They looked at each other with raised eyebrows, as Josh mouthed the word "Wow".

One of the other students, Tori Desjardins, raised her hand and the professor acknowledged her. Tori stood up.

"I understand that hospitality and service are really important," she started, "but I don't see how they could change my life." She paused for a moment to think as Josh looked around the room with many students nodding in agreement ... "Isn't that a little dramatic Professor?" She asked, and then softened her criticism with "If you don't mind me saying so?" And then she sat down to murmurs going around the room.

Professor Sydney paused thoughtfully, placing his hands on his desk. He chuckled softly. It was obvious he was restraining himself. He then replied to Tori, choosing his words carefully.

"If you do the Assignment the way it is intended, you will find that what you are about to experience in the field Assignment will open your eyes and give you new insights. That is what could change your life." He smiled at the Student as she bit on her pen, trying to hide her scepticism.

"You see," he continued with a patient tone in his voice that said he had heard this before, "I could stand here all semester" he continued, "Listing for you all the criteria for excellent service or I could have you read countless case studies and books on the subject. However, I have learned that the best teaching on this subject comes from the student experiencing various levels of service and subsequently analyzing those experiences."

"That is why, Miss Desjardins, the majority of your time in the first semester will be spent in the field. It is all explained in the Assignment, which I will be handing out to you shortly. If you have any questions or would like to discuss anything with me during the field work portion of your work, I will be in my office during your class hours."

Monica felt goose-bumps coming on ... maybe this wasn't going to work for her. After all, she came to school to learn, not to go out 'in the field'. She felt nervous. She looked over at Josh who appeared to be eager.

"Think of it as an eye-opening experience," Josh grinned.

"You, always the optimist." Before Monica could say any more, the Professor was ready to distribute the Assignment.

"Note that you will work in pairs. Your teammate will be the person sitting to your right."

Monica felt total relief. She and Josh would be working on the project together.

Josh elbowed her "You, always the worrier. See, it's going to be fine."

"Before you leave today," added the Professor, "I want you to remember this. I actually do not like the word 'Service'. It can evoke too many one-dimensional thoughts, so I call it 'Hospitality'. Actually, that word does not do this broad, in-depth subject any justice either. Service, hospitality, whatever you want to call it, is a multi-dimensional subject that has far greater importance than most people imagine. It is my hope that by the end of this course, the majority of you will have learned to see the true depth of this subject. I think you will find certain parts of this Assignment surprising."

The Professor snickered, "Yes, I think you are going to learn a great deal from this Assignment, as have many others before you."

With that, the class was over.

Josh was pensive for a moment--"That guy either really knows what he's doing or he's burst a few brain cells."

Off they went to get some lunch and read the Assignment.

# Chapter 3

## The Assignment

### *Field Assignment for Course: Hospitality & Service—Winning Over the Customer*

Monica read the Assignment aloud to Josh.

*Dear Students:*

*Because of funds from my educational trust, I have allotted $525.00 to each Pairing. You may spend this money on purchasing items of your choice. You will sign for $175.00 at each of three intervals. You are to come to my office to receive the funds. I will explain this further when you visit me for your first installment. Please do so between tomorrow and next Wednesday.*

*You will perform each visit together and there will be a minimum of six (6) visits, that is, three purchases each. However, If you visit a Restaurant together, that will be considered one visit each, leaving each of you with two further visits. I strongly recommend that one of your visits be to an eating establishment, since Service and Hospitality are essential factors in the Food & Beverage industry.*

*During and after each visit, you should assess the Service & Hospitality you have received, taking into consideration EVERYTHING that turned you on and turned you off about your Service experience. In other words, reflect upon what you thought was good or excellent and what was mediocre or average about each visit, always bearing in mind that your primary focus should be on Service and Hospitality and all relevant factors. It is up to you to determine what those factors are.*

*A visit does not have to be for a purchase. For example, you may visit a place to acquire information.*

*In such a case, you would assess the Service and Hospitality experience just as you would for a purchase. Or you may inquire about something using the phone, email or a letter, provided the experience is substantial and significant. If you are unsure if an idea is relevant, you may ask me.*

*You will take notes and together discuss the experience surrounding each purchase. For every extra visit and assessment over six, you will receive a $25.00 bonus up to a maximum of $75.00 extra per couple. However, your marks will be measured on the quality of your perceptions, not on the number of visits.*

*You will be writing a joint report on all of your Service & Hospitality Experiences, explaining what you have learned, referencing all visits. You will present this written report orally together. Some of you will present your reports to me while others will be chosen to present theirs to the class as a whole. I will be giving you instructions that are more detailed on this in a private meeting, after you have completed all of your visits.* ***Do not begin writing the report until you have met with me.***

***You have ten weeks to complete this Assignment.***

*My schedule is posted on the door to my office. You must come to my office to get your first installment of funds. I will then answer any further questions you may have. However, I will not serve you up any information on service and hospitality.*

*You should each draw on and learn from your Partner's insights during this field Assignment. I too hope to learn something new from your experiences.*

*This Assignment will be worth at least 50% of your final grade in May.*

***NOTE****—Cheating of any type will be considered grounds for a failing grade and could lead to the expulsion of the culprit from this university or, at the very least, recording of the offence on your school record. For example, documentation of a visit that never occurred would be considered gross cheating. Consider me a relentless hound for such breaches of trust.*

*Secondly, I expect you to bring me your receipts at the three intervals mentioned earlier. At the end of your sojourn, you should also return any remaining funds with a record of your expenditures.*

*I suggest you review these instructions periodically to stay on track.*

*All the best to each of you in this endeavour. I encourage you to work hard and intelligently on this project.*

*It will serve you well.*

*Julius E. Sydney—Ph.D.*
*Professor & Dept. Head*
*School of Business*
*New Horizons University*

Monica gulped. "I have to reread this. Holy Mother of Mary!"

Josh stared out the window, wondering how he was going to cope. He knew that he and Monica were capable of producing great results, if they could get it together.

# Chapter 4

## Fighting Fear

***"Perfection is not attainable but if we chase perfection we can catch excellence."***

***Vince Lombardi***

After Monica quietly reread the instructions for the Assignment, she placed her head between her hands. "Josh, I don't know if I can do this! It's going to be way harder than I thought."

Josh hadn't seen Monica this rattled in some time. He knew what he had to do. "Hey there, where's that competitive spirit....c'mon Monns. You love challenges. Assignments always sound worse than they are; you know that. We just need to break it down into manageable steps and then it won't seem so overpowering. And besides, I need you! We're in this whole thing together."

Monica managed an awkward, lopsided smile. She didn't want to let Josh down. She knew he was right about breaking down the Assignment into manageable steps.

"Mind you," Josh said pensively, "It seems to me that we should be reading some books before we venture into the field of service."

That comment caught Monica's attention.

"I see where the Professor is coming from on that point," Monica felt herself regaining her inner strength. She had written down

some of the Professor's words and now paused to read them:-
***-"If you want to learn how splendid service and hospitality can change your life and the lives of others, then stick around and prepare yourself to learn and be the better for it. That is the power of outstanding service."***

Monica knew at that moment that she wanted to learn what the Professor meant.

***"Think about it JJ. Sure, if you're in the service business, a good book on the subject can be really helpful--you know, books by experts, by successful business people--they can teach people how they can improve their operation. But we're supposed to be Customers and you can't teach a Customer how they are supposed to feel when they're being served. You can't teach a Customer how to behave. A Customer is happy, lukewarm or dissatisfied with their service experience. You can't program a Customer. I think a field Assignment is right on actually!"***

"Bravo!" cheered Josh. "The Girl is back! Brilliant speech or should I say diatribe!"

"Oh, shush up JJ. You're a menace to society." Monica mischievously grabbed a notebook to whack Josh's head.

"I see you're feeling better," laughed Josh while protecting his head.

"Phew, I lost it there for a minute. Let's go for a walk, OK?" asked Monica

"At your SERVICE ma'am!" Josh opened the door.

Monica smiled, "Thanks...and for the pep talk too."

Josh gave her that wink that came across as if he was saying both "my pleasure" and "no problem" at the same time. The breeze felt so good on their faces. They breathed in the clean fresh air, walking and talking about everything and nothing.

# Chapter 5

## The First Escapade--Part 1

***"If you build a great experience, customers tell each other about that. Word of mouth is very powerful."***

***Jeff Bezos—Founder, Amazon***

"So, where does the Lady wish to dine this evening?" enquired Josh, while wiping a bench for Monica.

"Oh my, I feel like royalty. Well Sir, I've heard that Jardin C'eleste is heavenly."

"Uhum, and anywhere else m'lady? Josh loved to imitate various British dialects.

" I would say either Jardin C'eleste or Kat's Seafood Paradise. Kat's sounds tropical. I'm edging towards Kat's Seafood. But either one, or if you know or have a place you want to try, whatever, really. I'm just excited to go and judge Service and gorge myself with yummy food!"

"We shall go with Kat's, as the Lady wishes, for 7:30pm? I'll drop you off and then..."

"No, no, that's OK. I have some things to pick up and I have no idea what I'm going to wear tonight. I'll see you at 7:15. I'll be waiting outside. I'm so ready for this! See you soon Shakespeare," she sang.

Monica's excitement was tempered with some inner apprehension. Concerned that any sign of uncertainty could eclipse their evening, she had not mentioned her nervousness to Josh. Understanding their relationship very well, Monica knew she should be the one to come up with a plan of action for their upcoming Visits. Planning was one of her strengths and Josh, well he was more of a carpe diem kind of Guy. As she walked, she could feel ideas coming together. In the meantime, there was a good deal of personal preparation ahead plus a few items to pick up on her way home, like nail polish and a special Journal for documentation.

Josh, on the other hand, was bothered by another kind of worry. He had not been spending as much time with Bean. Josh was feeling the weight of the winds of guilt hover over him, the kind of guilt that parents, especially single parents, feel when they have been away or out a lot. Josh just wanted the feeling to disappear. However, he realized that the best he could do was try not to think about it during dinner. After all, he reflected, Maureen was coming over to stay with Bean; it wasn't as if he was leaving Bean with a stranger. He then pictured Bean having fun with his Aunt Mau. That image eased his mind somewhat.

As Monica prepared for the evening, she tried on just about every dress she owned. Finally, she decided on the red one. It had been some time since Monica had gone out for a special evening. Although she was anxious, tonight she felt a sense of optimism and excitement that had eluded her since her last break up. She took one final look in the mirror and fussed a bit with her hair and makeup, until she felt satisfied with her appearance. She laughed a little as she took a full turn in front of the mirror. "I feel like a debutante," she told her reflection. "Monica Janine Flowers, you're going to have a dreamy evening."

It was a balmy evening but there was a nippy breeze. Josh arrived right on time. Monica was wearing a black and white Pashmina shawl. His eyes popped as she slid into the front seat.

"You look beautiful!" Now how am I supposed to study the Service when you look like that!"

Monica felt flattered. "You look pretty spiffy yourself, Sir." After a few moments of being settled, they chatted about the great weather and how famished they both were. Josh amused and taunted Monica with some food jokes.

After a few more minutes, Monica decided that now was a good time to bring up the subject of a strategy for their upcoming Service assessments.

"I've been thinking about how we'd do this," she began. Josh raised his brow. "How we would go about assessing service and hospitality for each of our visits," explained Monica. You know, having a system that we can use for each one."

"Why don't we just see how it goes. Let's enjoy the process, starting with this evening. Then we can talk about our strategy." Josh was in no mood for any intense conversation. Bean was still on his mind, among other things.

"Josh, don't patronize me. Trust me when I say we shouldn't just wing it for our first visit. It's really important. We need to be on the same page for this. That's what partners and teammates do, right? They support each other and discuss things to reach a solution that they both feel good about."

"I didn't mean to upset you. I just really want us to have a happy evening. We both deserve it."

"And I just want us to do well. To me this Assignment is like an adventure." Before Josh could get a word in edgewise, Monica was eager to explain. "OK, so here's what I was thinking. First we observe the Service and the Hospitality, then we point out our observations to each other as we see or hear things that grab our attention—like behavior of the People serving us, anything that impresses or turns us off. After we talk about each point, we write down the things that we noticed and any epiphanies either of us may have. See, I bought this hard-covered red book; it has blank pages so we can use it as our Journal. Then, after each visit, we do a kind of debriefing—in other words, we dissect it, analyse, scrutinize, talk about the strengths, weaknesses and draw conclusions. We jot down the conclusions that come out of our discussion. That's just a rough summary but I think it makes sense. So, what do you think?" Monica was on the edge of her seat. She wondered if Josh was even listening.

"Makes sense to me too. Okay, high five?" Josh put his right hand up. "That's what we'll do then. See how easy I am to get along with?" Josh's enthusiasm was returning.

"High five!" laughed Monica. "You had me going there for a minute. Really, you think that's good?"

"Actually, it sounds like a great plan. I think it would work really well to have the Journal. Those notes have to turn into a good analysis of three things though: What customers think, What they want and thirdly, How to give it to them." Josh was starting to feel more committed. "Also," he continued, "I'm all for a good plan but leave some room for improvising along the way, like finding out why it's important to give customers great service."

"Right, I will. First you're a mule and then you're Einstein! Those three points are perfect!"

Monica opened their Journal to the first page and wrote,

***OUR MISSION:***
***A. What Customers Think***
***B. What they Want***
***C. How to Give it to Them***

"Those three points will be like a guide for us JJ. See what happens when we figure things out together. Hey, there's a sign....'For Kat's, Enter here'." Josh turned into a rather narrow laneway. It was just beginning to get dark. The laneway was well lit, as was the sign, 'Welcome to Kat's Seafood Paradise'.

The building was a mixture of stone and cedar. The roof had three high peaks. "Rustic with a modern look", was the way Monica described it.

As they entered the large foyer, there was a lineup almost to the door, about fifteen deep. It was a Thursday night.

"Wow, this place must be popular. Looks like we made a good choice." Josh made his way to the booking desk.

"Excuse me," he said, as he approached the desk. "I made a reservation for 7:30pm for Johnson and Flowers."

"Wonderful to see you both. We have a very nice table by the window ready for you." The Maître D smiled warmly as she led the couple to their table.

"I love the feel of this place already," whispered Monica as she held Josh's arm. The Couple followed the Maître D to their table, gazing here and there. She smiled and wished them a very pleasurable evening.

Monica could not help but look everywhere. "Wow Josh.....it's quite the place! I think we chose well."

"Remember my Sweet; we're here to assess service, not to look at the scenery."

"For your information the scenery, as you call it, is a really important part of both service and hospitality. Serving us up great atmosphere makes a big difference in how a place makes a person feel. I mean if we came in and the tables were a mess and the decors consisted of four painted walls, how would you feel then about where we came to have a special dinner? I for one wouldn't feel very welcome or comfortable." Monica was visibly proud of her explanation.

"You're on fire Girl! I never thought of that. Great point! When the Girl's right, she's right," Josh added flirtatiously. "Ambience is really important, I must admit. I don't know what I was thinking. "

"I love a man who knows how to admit when he's wrong," responded Monica playfully. "It's kind of enchanting here--

really classy but so comfortable." She took it all in with a deep breath.

Josh was thrilled that Monica liked the venue so much. He felt relieved. It was important to him that their service escapades began on a positive note.

As the two were drawn to watch the fish in the aquarium, a nice-looking, very tall fellow was approaching their table, dressed in a crisp white shirt and stylish black pants.

"Hi, I'm Andy, very sorry to keep you waiting. Your Server, Ashleigh, asked me to take your beverage orders, that is, if you're ready."

Monica noticed his name badge said 'Manager'.

"Oh gosh," said Monica, somewhat embarrassed. "We've been too busy chatting and admiring your Restaurant to...so sorry to hold you up."

"Not at all a problem Ms. Flowers. We're on your time, not ours. Please do take your time. Either Ashleigh or I will be back to take your drink order or your full order, whichever you wish and whenever YOU are ready," he smiled assuredly. As he left their table, they began to browse through the cocktail menu.

When Andy was out of earshot distance, Monica piped up, "OK, right there, right there Josh...did you see that? He's a manager or The Manager...who knows....and he came over because one of his Servers was really busy...now I call that SERVICE and HOSPITALITY. And what he said, "We're on your time, not ours." Wow, talk about making a person feel relaxed and at ease."

"I've never heard that one before either. Impressive and real Teamwork. The Guy was sincere too. He wasn't faking it. I could tell," Josh commented.

"We've got to write these things down," said Monica reaching for their Journal.

The Couple then focused on their drink menus for a few moments. Both commented that they liked the layout of the menus and how the ingredients for each cocktail were listed. As they looked up, there was an attractive blonde woman, with a white blouse and black skirt at their table, ready to take their beverage order. This was Ashleigh.

"Hi, Ms. Flowers, Mr. Johnson. I'm Ashleigh and I'll be looking after you this evening. By the way, I love your dress Ms. Flowers" Monica was delighted. "May I get you a starting beverage from our spectacular bar?"

Drinks were ordered and the couple returned to gazing at the decors. They both felt very relaxed. By the time Ashleigh returned with their drinks, Josh's worries about Bean had disappeared.

Umm…oh my, wow… this drink is so yummy and I love the glasses," noted Monica. "They're classy but cool-looking too. And Ashleigh is so sweet. She has kind, beautiful eyes. How's your drink Josh?"

"Ya, she really seems like a pleasant person, relaxed but enjoys people. My drink is really good. Thumbs up on the drinks and the service so far," raved Josh, raising his glass.

"I've already learned something that I think we should put in our report." Just as Monica was going to share her thoughts, Ashleigh approached the table with a big smile. Josh and Monica were each ready to order. They were both famished.

# Chapter 6

## *The First Escapade--Part 2*

After Ashleigh answered their questions, the duo each ordered a salad, the Seafood Platter for Two and a bottle of the red Italian wine, chosen by Monica.

"What were you saying before Moni, about what we should put in our report?"

Monica wanted to express her revelation just right. She paused, took a breath, then took a few slow sips of her drink, as she gathered her thoughts.

Before Monica had time to speak, Josh excused himself for a moment. When he returned, he seemed electrified. "You have to see the full aquarium. It's amazing! It extends all around the corner. This place is shaped sort of like a kidney. You have to see this!" Josh grabbed Monica's hand.

The aquarium was teeming with life and colour.

"Wow, look at all those beautiful fish....I could watch them all night," gleamed Monica.

Then, as they turned, the Twosome couldn't believe they hadn't noticed the greenery all around the Restaurant, intertwined with bamboo lattice borders. It must have been the soft lighting," said Josh. "Otherwise, how could we have missed all this!"

"I feel like we're in Tahiti or something!" swooned Monica, while admiring the decor.

The floors were made of dark wooden planks and the walls looked like logs made of cedar. There were tribal-like artifacts all over in bright colours...orange, coral and lime-green. Some of the vase-shaped containers had Mardi-Gras style beads draped around them.

Monica was totally mesmerized. "The decor is so inviting and almost seductive. I saw this movie that took place in a town called Paradise, in Massachusetts. At the beginning of the movie, they had the definition of the word 'paradise' and it said it was a place of 'ideal beauty'. This place is like a little paradise."

As Josh and Monica headed back to their table, they noticed a sign, which was obviously very old, perhaps from a flea market somewhere. It read "Eat Well and Be Happy."

They returned to their table, still smiling from reading the sign. They also noticed that all the tables but one were taken.

"I like the way they have arranged the tables so that people aren't packed together," remarked Josh. In some places the tables are so close together, you feel as if you're having dinner with the people on either side of you!"

Monica laughed. "I noticed that too, JJ. And I like how everyone in the Restaurant gets a view of the main attraction, the aquarium. And the fish seem so at home and healthy. It's a really clean aquarium too. My parents use to have an aquarium and they are not easy to look after. This one is awesome!"

By the time Monica and Josh had returned to their table, their wine and salads were waiting for them.

Ashleigh spotted them and poured the wine after Monica

completed the tasting. "I love your centre pieces Ashleigh. They're earthy & elegant."

Ashleigh smiled, "They were made locally by a super-talented amateur potter. So glad you like them."

"She's so nice," said Monica as she took her first bite of salad. She closed her eyes and breathed in, as if she had tasted heaven on earth.

"JJ, I love how this place makes me feel--it's classy but really relaxing and comfortable. Even the chairs are comfortable. I love how the orange upholstery matches the orange pottery. Everything's really well thought out. Did you know orange is a happy colour?"

"A happy colour?" Josh look confused but he was thrilled that Monica was having a great time.

"Uhuh. See, every colour has a kind of energy that creates a mood and the colour orange is for fun, happiness and confidence," explained Monica, who was obviously experiencing all of those sensations.

Hunger had taken over Josh's hearing as he dug into his salad. Neither Monica nor Josh had eaten lunch. Monica repeatedly made 'mm…mm' sounds with almost every bite.

During the silence they enjoyed the Indie music that was playing. It was relaxing yet upbeat.

"I like the music," mentioned Josh.

"I thought you didn't like Indie music?" teased Monica, helping herself to a bite of Josh's salad.

"Well, I like it tonight! It kind of goes with the atmosphere and everything."

Once their salads were finished, Josh raised his wine glass, this time to propose a toast. "To the best and prettiest Pal a guy could ask for." Monica lifted her glass to his and added, "Here's to eating well and being happy." At that moment, both felt extra grateful for their long-time friendship.

"OK Ms. Flowers, what's your big revelation?" asked Josh. "Now that we have some food in our tummies, I'd like to digest it with some Monica genius.

"You would, would you?" Monica had written down some of her thoughts but there was one point in particular that she believed to be a real revelation.

Ashleigh arrived, carrying their Seafood Platter.

"Oh my, this is a veritable feast! I love the presentation!" Monica hesitated taking the first piece but Josh insisted.

"I like the pacing....they don't rush you and it's not too slow either...pretty right on with the timing," mentioned Josh, as he was choosing which piece of seafood he would try next.

As they ate their dinner, the two enjoyed every morsel. Josh's worries were far from his mind as he chatted with Monica over dinner. They tried to stay focused on service and what they saw going on around them. They both felt relaxed and satisfied and when they swayed off topic, Monica brought them back with an observation. They both felt as if they were noticing things about Service that were important, features and factors that neither of them had ever paid much attention to before.

Hey Josh, "Don't you think that Ashleigh is just made for this profession? I mean she's so into it and the way she serves all her tables and never seems to get flustered. That takes a lot of composure and concentration. She has great instincts to, as if she anticipates what the customer needs even before they ask. There's this genuine sincerity about her. I also like the way she takes her time at the table, with Customers, and then moves fast to get things done. That shows a real desire to make the Customer happy. Boy, I bet she gets great tips and well-deserved I say."

"For sure. And kudos to the Management too," nodded Josh. Did you notice how the Servers and the Managers help each other, without any hesitation? It's as if the teamwork is contagious. It's almost too good to be true but here it is. It's like everyone is watching out for each other. The energy is amazing."

"The energy," uttered Monica slowly. That's a really important concept Josh."

"What is?"

"What you just said about the energy being amazing. It's a key point. I'm writing that down. That's why I felt so good when I walked in. It's the feeling this place gives you. It gives off a really wonderful energy that makes you want to stay here."

Ashleigh then stopped by to check on the Couple. "Looks as if you're enjoying everything." Ashleigh glanced all over their table and then waited for Josh and Monica's response.

Both nodded with their mouths full, in a way that let Ashleigh know they were loving it. "Oh, I'm so glad you like everything," she beamed. "Just wave if you need anything."

"MONICA....YOUR BIG REVELATION? TELL ME!" insisted Josh.

# Chapter 7

## *Scratching the Surface*

"OK, it may sound like a simple observation but it's one I never stopped to realize before. Actually, there are two important things. Ashleigh inspired me to see these themes."

Monica cleared her throat and could not resist another sip of wine before she explained: "First, The person serving has to Think Like *They* Are The Customer Being Served. Even things like layout and wording of the menus…you know? They have to put themselves in the Customer's shoes for real. Maybe everyone wouldn't admit it but the truth is, when you're a Customer, you want to feel as if you really matter! So, the two things I've written down are, ***'THINK LIKE THE CUSTOMER YOU ARE SERVING'*** and ***'MAKE THAT CUSTOMER FEEL LIKE THEY REALLY MATTER'***. It sounds so simple but it isn't. It takes a special knack. Some people have that ability and others have to be willing to learn it."

'Ya, those are good observations Monns but aren't they kind of elementary? 'Thinking like a Customer' is just another way of saying the Golden Rule…. the 'do unto others….' message. And of course Customers want to feel like they matter. Tell me something I don't know. I don't mean to be harsh but I think our analysis has to be more profound than that."

"Here's a question Josh. Do you feel appreciated in this Restaurant?"

"Yes, I do actually."

"WELL, I THINK THAT'S BECAUSE ASHLEIGH, THE MANAGER AT THE BEGINNING, AND JUST THE WHOLE AMBIENCE OF THE PLACE HAS MADE US FEEL SPECIAL, LIKE WE REALLY MATTER. THAT, JOSH, IS WHAT GREAT SERVICE IS SUPPOSED TO BE LIKE! AND, FOR YOUR INFORMATION, SOME OF THE GREATEST THINKERS IN HISTORY HAD A KNACK FOR EXPRESSING CRITICAL, COMPLEX THOUGHTS IN SIMPLE TERMS."

"I hate to rain on your parade Sweety. It's true the service tonight has been excellent. But how many times in your life have you experienced service like this? I mean this just is not the kind of service I've received most of my life and I bet it's the same for you and most people."

"Joshua, why are you being so negative?"

"I'm not being negative. I'm being real. I mean most people in service aren't all that enthused about serving people, to put it mildly, or at least that's the way they act. Maybe they're trying to be cool or maybe they just don't care but that's the reality."

Monica was determined to make her point. "Listen, it's not just Ashleigh who is so upbeat and on the ball, It's all of the people who work here. When we were walking through, even the people in the kitchen seemed to get along really well with each other and with the Servers. They really seem to understand and like each other."

"Maybe the Owner or whoever does the hiring just has a good eye for people who would be good at Service. Who knows?" suggested Josh casually.

Ashleigh stopped by to pick up the Couple's plates and asked if they would like to see a dessert menu. "It looks as if you two enjoyed your meal," said Ashleigh looking at the empty platter.

"It was sooo good Ashleigh!" replied Monica.

"Really great food....thank the Chef for us," added Josh.

The Twosome ordered coffee and a caramel sundae with two spoons.

"We have to talk this through JJ. We have to figure out why these people are so great at what they do and why they obviously care so much about their Customers. True, good hiring is important but there's more to it than that. The places where I have worked in service have had real problems finding good people, so I don't think the attitude in this place can be explained away by good hiring only. I just know there's more to it than that. And if tips were the only motivation, well then all servers in all restaurants who receive tips, would be doing an excellent job at service. But that is not the case, is it?"

"That's true. So why do the People in this place understand and execute service so well. That's what we need to understand. We have to go deeper Monns. Nice little phrases like "Think like a Customer" are just that, nice little phrases that don't make a big difference."

Monica rolled her eyes at Josh and pointed her spoon directly at him as she responded. "How do you know that nice little phrases don't have some impact, oh cynical one, hum? You're saying you don't think that a certain philosophy in a workplace makes a difference? Is that what you're saying? Because if it is, I strongly disagree."

Just then, Ashleigh stopped by with two champagne glasses and two tiny individual-sized bottles of champagne.

"This is just a little gift from our Manager. This particular champagne is perfect for the end of the meal. I hope you enjoy it."

Monica was speechless, as Josh thanked Ashleigh for the kind gesture."

"It's the little things....like this. Wow!" Monica was caught by surprise. Josh was suitably impressed.

"Oh my, this is so good. Josh, taste it. You know, it's the little things and they come from thinking like a Customer."

"It is the little things," agreed Josh, raising his glass to Monica's. "Here's to life's little pleasures vis-a-vis Kat's Paradise."

"Man, this has been awesome. Are you enjoying yourself Sweety?"

"It's one of the best evenings I've had in a very long time. And you?"

"Same here...I'd say it was a very successful first visit in ALL ways.

Once they had finished their coffee and champagne, Josh and Monica thanked Ashleigh and left her a 20% tip. Ashleigh brought back Josh's card and smiled warmly at both of them. "It really has been a pleasure serving you. I hope you will come back to see us. People like you make my job so enjoyable." She then laid down some peppermint chocolate with something written on the back of a business card and thanked Josh and Monica once again before leaving their table. The note read, "You are a beautiful couple".

"What a thoughtful thing to do...really lovely touch," murmured Monica.

The Twosome entered the foyer where the Maître D helped Monica with her shawl and wished the Couple a lovely evening, adding that Ashleigh had mentioned how much she enjoyed serving them.

As they left the restaurant Monica lamented, "I feel as if I am leaving Paradise." She spent the drive quietly reflecting about their evening. It gave her goose bumps. Josh was also quiet as they listened to some music.

"That was really a sumptuous experience in every way JJ —way better than I had imagined. Did I mention how spotless and beautiful the washroom was!"

"Ya, it was really wonderful, wasn't it—very special, way better than I expected. Now for the fun part, the debriefing," winked Josh.

"Ha, ha...yes, this should be very interesting....our collaboration, our synthesis, our...oh, we're here already," beamed the woman in the red dress.

# Chapter 8

## Monica's Defence

***"Be a yardstick of quality. Some people aren't used to an environment where excellence is expected."***

***Steve Jobs***

After putting Bean to bed, Monica joined Josh in the kitchen where he was preparing some tea.

"Thanks, I really need this. I ate so much," she sighed. "Phew, I'm not used to feeling so satisfied."

"By the way, my excellent tea-maker, you're wrong you know—what did you call them? I think it was 'nice little phrases'—when you said that they don't do anything to inspire change."

Josh placed Monica's tea next to her. "How so? I didn't mean any offence by it. That's just been my experience. People forget phrases or they stop meaning something."

"See the thing is Josh, when we generalize like that—and believe me, I do it too—we can really miss some 'nice little phrases'. The written word, when lifted from the page, can and has changed attitudes and events. For example, listen to this one: ***'I go forth alone and stand as ten-thousand'***. What do you think of that line?"

"Wow, it's powerful, kind of hits you in the gut. Who said that?"

"Maya Angelou, have you heard of her? It's a line from her poem, 'Our Grandmothers'."

"Have I heard of her? Are you kidding me! I watched her on TV at Bill Clinton's first inauguration with my parents. I was too young to understand her poem but just her presence and her voice made a huge impression on me. I think every black person in America who watched it must have felt so proud to see her standing there! Wow, 'I go forth alone and stand as ten thousand'. Really makes you think about the power of one individual."

"In your own way, you did that with Bean, when you decided to take on the responsibility of becoming a single Dad. That took courage JJ. A lot of guys would never have taken that on."

Monica continued, "Think of some of the great poetry and great quotations, not to mention biblical proverbs--some people live their lives by those words. So to me, it's about the power of the phrase and HOW it is put to use. People need to feel committed to some kind of philosophy. That's only one factor but it's a factor that can't just be generalized as 'nice little phrases'. I think most people crave something to believe in. Why not give them that at work too?"

Josh's eyes were focused on Monica. "Are you saying that you think the type of service and teamwork at Kat's Restaurant was because of some powerful philosophy that everyone there bought into?"

"I'm saying that had to be part of it. Perhaps that's where you start when you want to inspire people. That's where most great leaders begin. And there's another thing--great service and hospitality requires inspiring leadership. Someone's got to point the way, right?"

"That's true," reflected Josh aloud. Look at Barack Obama's ***'Yes We Can'***!" A whole nation of downhearted people bought into that and he became the first African-American President in U.S. history! The economy was in turmoil and here was this African-American Senator saying 'Yes we Can' make things better, together. It was magical. I sure would have voted for him, no matter what colour he was."

"And how about Pierre Elliott Trudeau's ***'Just Society'***?" added Monica. "That was his platform and he won and became one of the most popular Prime Minister's in Canadian history, using two words! I mean, as I read about it, those two words were the essence of his whole campaign and he won big. In fact, he became a global celebrity. He was charismatic and believable so when he promised a Just Society, people ate it up."

"Pierre Elliott Trudeau! That was well before your time Monns."

"I like history. I learn from it. Did you know that Trudeau's 'Just Society' the *Charter of Rights* and the *Human Rights Act* brought huge changes that have influenced so many of the attitudes and rights in this Country, as well as things like the *Young Offenders Act*? That one's being revised right now by Prime Minister Harper and..."

"Wow! No, I didn't know all that. It sounds way more interesting than I thought it was. If I can just get back to the quotations--I thought they were really powerful. See, the words in those quotations stayed with people and made them feel something. There's a big difference between those quotations and the phrase, 'Thinking Like a Customer'...just saying'. Don't be mad."

"How about this one Mr. Cynical: ***'To understand the man, you must first walk a mile in his moccasin'***," Monica stated, peering at Josh.

"I like that. I'll remember that one. Who said it?"

"It's a North American Indian Proverb and I bet you that all First Nations People and Native Americans know it too. Now, does that sound to you like anything I've been saying?" asked Monica with her brows raised.

"Your 'Think like a Customer' means the same thing—put yourself in the other person's moccasins."

"Uh-huh, but for some people, "Think like a Customer' might sound new and fresh, just like the Indian Proverb did to you. JJ, are you listening?"

"Yes, I am but I was thinking that obviously it depends on who your audience is. That may work for some people but…"

"Right, I agree," interrupted Monica. "You have to know what level of expertise and understanding your people are at. And you have to know what words will really motivate them. The words must have genuine meaning to employees so they FEEL the words. Motivation comes from feeling something, being inspired. Three simple words, 'Yes We Can', worked for a whole country. Obama believed it and he made millions of people believe it right along with him. That is what a great leader does."

Josh had changed his mind. "OK, so there has to be a philosophy, one that Employees buy into. Plus, the philosophy needs an unconditional commitment from all Managers and has be practised by them to inspire the Staff. Is that basically what you're saying?"

"Basically, yes but the 'how'—the how is really important. I once worked for a Company and they sat all the Managers in a meeting room and said we should all come up with a mission statement. Presumably, if we came up with the statement together, in this meeting, we would all buy into it."

"So what happened?" asked Josh.

"Well, we came up with a mission statement. It went something like 'We're here to Please You'. But not much changed after that. It was like it was class and then our task was done."

"So what are you saying Monns. First you say, there should be a mission statement and then you say it doesn't work?"

"Hold on. I'll explain. See, the people in the room who liked it, well they were the least committed managers but in that room, they were also the most articulate ones. The most committed managers weren't wordsmiths. They were just great Managers. So what I'm saying is let the visionary, hopefully the Owner or GM or a Manager who is truly committed, or both together, come up with the words, because they're more likely to be able to communicate and execute the vision to everyone else. Here's the clipper—it has to be someone who is either charismatic or believable or someone who is passionate and inspiring. And that person has to be hungry. They have to have the energy and the desire to inspire others. First that person gets a buy-in from one or two people and then it spreads. Those who don't get it, well bye-bye!"

"Right," agreed Josh. Well, obviously the People who work at Kat's Seafood Paradise understand how critical service and hospitality are. You know, it seemed to me that when Ashleigh made us happy, that made her genuinely happy. Now if you could sell that concept to employees--'MAKE A CUSTOMER HAPPY AND YOU WILL FEEL AWESOME'-- if they could experience that feeling, then you could actually change people. Whatever concept they have a Kat's, it's working. It didn't just happen overnight. It started with somebody inspiring those people and at least one other person who bought into it."

"Yes! YOU GOT IT. JOSH GOT IT!! Monica felt euphoric and Josh, well, he was obviously uplifted and inspired by the whole conversation.

# Chapter 9

## Josh's Transformation

***"Knowing is not enough; we must apply.
Willing is not enough; we must do."***

***Bruce Lee***

When Josh finished writing some notes in their Journal, he was anxious to share his own thoughts and views with Monica.

He began, "I really think you hit on something Monns. But one thing that really struck me was that the Staff were working in a really nice place, right? I mean as a workplace it had a lot going for it. The upkeep was excellent; it was clean, and, then there's that incredible aquarium and if you worked there, that set up with the aquarium and all, it would have a soothing and overall positive effect, not to mention the greenery. Actually, it was the whole package really. I bet the tips are pretty good too. I mean, who wouldn't want to work there?"

Monica was on her feet. "Who wouldn't want to work there? Are you kidding me?! How about people who don't want to work hard or people who only care about themselves and have no clue or savvy about teamwork OR people who would find it too stressful? How many times have you heard a co-worker say, "oh, I'm so stressed out," as if they're threatening to quit. Kat's was really busy and they definitely were not overstaffed—just the opposite. How many people can do that and make it look easy, eh Josh? Give those people some credit. I mean sure, it was a great-looking place and prestigious but how many people can hack that? Sure, no doubt they get their share of applications but that's because the Managers, Servers, Chefs, Maître D...everyone there...make it look easy. So tell me Josh, how many people have you worked with who could exert that kind of effort willingly and with a genuine smile, make it look easy and treat customers as if they were the only people on earth who mattered?! Answer that one for me. Oh sure, lots of people may want to work there but only the very few could cut it. Let's face it, there's no easy road to financial success, unless you win a lottery."

Monica sat down and took a deep breath. "Furthermore" she continued, "Have you noticed lately how many wealthy celebrities still continue to work? I think it's because people who are self-motivated don't just do it for the money. They do it because they enjoy that feeling of accomplishing something other than wealth. The feeling of accomplishment is like a drug. Once you've tasted it, you want more. I bet the Servers at Kat's could take a nice vacation with the tips they make. But oh my, the road to that vacation is NOT an easy one my Friend."

"Holy Mother Theresa Monica! That was quite a rant but..." "A rant, a rant Josh! That's all you got out of what I said? Maybe I have the wrong partner for this. You can be so immature." Monica was close to tears but controlled herself and remained resolute.

"Hold up Monica! What I was going to say was that, as much as it pains me to agree with you, you're right. I know that because I used to be just like that--thought I could do a job the easy way, you know, be cool. I've always been a dependable working stiff but I never tried to stand out--okay, maybe I tried really hard as a Dad but not at work. I say dumb things sometimes. You deserve better. What you said really did penetrate my pea brain."

"Sorry about the rant JJ. I just feel very strongly about it. It's like the title of the book by Jim Donovan, *This is Your Life, Not a Dress Rehearsal*. You have to grab onto it with everything you've got!"

"I shouldn't have called it a rant. It was more like a dynamic discourse. You should be a motivational speaker-- Monica Janine Flowers, Motivational Speaker extraordinaire. I bow to your prowess. I'm not kidding. Your passion, that's what I need more of. I envy the way you care so much."

"I appreciate that JJ. Now let's keep going with this. So, let me ask you this, if the experience at Kat's hadn't been as good as you expected, would you go back and give them a second chance?"

"Probably not, not at those prices anyway. If I'm going to have to stretch my wallet, then the service, the food, the atmosphere, and the whole hospitality thing, have to surpass my expectations. I want to be surprised at how great the whole experience is. It should stand out from other experiences. You know, there have been many times when I've spent money and haven't felt like it was worth it. At Kat's, it was worth it. There was value for my dollar. I felt like I got more than what I paid for. I think the value point is really important. IT'S NOT ABOUT THE COST. IT'S ABOUT FEELING AS IF YOU GOT MORE THAN WHAT YOU PAID FOR. That's what 'value' means to me and I think it means that to most people."

"Fantastic point! I've got to write that in the Journal." Monica wrote:

- ***BETTER THAN EXPECTED SERVICE ADDS VALUE and BRINGS THEM BACK.***
- ***VALUE MEANS FEELING AS IF YOU GOT MORE THAN WHAT YOU PAID FOR.***

JOSH WAS UP ON HIS FEET AS IF HE HAD AN EPIPHANY. HE REPEATED THE IDEA AS HE PACED. "OK, 'BETTER THAN EXPECTED SERVICE ADDS VALUE AND BRINGS THEM BACK'--THAT REALLY IS THE KEY MONNS. IF CUSTOMERS COME BACK, THAT INCREASES SALES AND IF SALES INCREASE, THERE'S MORE CASH FLOW AND PROFITS FOR THE OWNERS, AND IF THAT IS THE CASE, THEN THEY CAN ENHANCE THE APPEARANCE OF THEIR ESTABLISHMENT, HIRE THE RIGHT PEOPLE AND PAY THEM MORE. WHAT BETTER

WAY TO ADD VALUE TO A CUSTOMER'S VISIT THAN THROUGH EXCELLENCE IN SERVICE! EVERYBODY WINS!"

"High five Genius!" cheered Monica. "Josh, you're being passionate...see, you can be that guy you want to be."

"Monns, I want to make a difference. It sounds cliché but I really do. No matter what I do, I want to do it really well, you know? I don't want to waste my time being average anymore."

"See Josh, that's the difference between people like you and the person who doesn't care or the person who figures that average effort is good enough or the guy who figures he's already good enough."

MONICA THOUGHT FOR A MOMENT. "I REALLY THINK THAT THE FIRST STEP TO EXCELLENCE IN ANYTHING IS THAT YOU HAVE TO WANT TO DO AN EXCELLENT JOB. IF YOU DON'T TAKE PRIDE IN YOUR WORK, THEN YOU DON'T TAKE PRIDE IN YOURSELF. THAT'S JUST BASIC. YOU HAVE TO WANT TO TAKE PRIDE IN YOURSELF. THAT'S NOT AN EASY THING TO DO SOMETIMES. IT MEANS BEING STRONG, NOT LETTING THE LAZY SIDE OF YOU TAKE OVER AND NOT LISTENING TO NEGATIVE PEOPLE WHO MAKE EXCUSES AND KNOCK EVERYONE ELSE BUT THEMSELVES."

"True and well said. But in the real world a lot of people are pulled down by their circumstances," maintained Josh.

"Yes, but also in the real world, as you like to call it, a lot of people pull themselves up and rise above their circumstances, like both of our Parents for example. What about that?"

Josh looked at Monica with a smile that spelled admiration. She had made a strong point. "You're right Monns; you are so very right. I just want to add that it really helps if the training is done well, by someone who is a stellar employee, a role model type of person, someone who is a champion at heart, you know, a person who other employees look up to."

Josh chuckled, "I remember this email someone sent to me with all sorts of clever sayings. The one I liked best was: ***'I thought I wanted a career. Turns out I just wanted paychecks'***. "

"Ha-ha, I like that…It's like one of those discovery sayings that make you really look at yourself and what kind of person you are and want to be."

"Not so funny. That used to be me," lamented Josh.

"Like you just said JJ, 'used to be' you—past tense."

"Monica, you don't see how different you are from most other people. They just have a good laugh at a statement like that. Most of them never take a statement like that and think about what kind of person they are or want to be. I read this book called, *Who Moved My Cheese*? by Spencer Johnson. I'm pretty sure that's his name. He showed how people want to protect who they are. Most people don't like change. I guess that's why it's taken me this long to come face to face with my own weaknesses. Cause once you do that, you have a choice, a choice to either change for the better or just go with who you are. Man, what a great night."

As Josh was driving Monica home, she felt they had really learned and accomplished a lot that evening. However, she noticed that something was bothering Josh. "Hey there, everything OK JJ?"

"Ya, sorry. I was just thinking. Here I am talking with you about people giving their all to their work. I didn't."

"You didn't what?" asked Monica puzzled.

"If I had given to my jobs the kind of focus and hard work that someone like Ashleigh gives to hers, I'd be somewhere by now. I feel like I was a loser. I should have at least gotten trained in a trade or something."

"Josh, that goes for both of us but look at us now? We're focused. We're trying harder. We're giving our new life everything we've got. We're in charge of our behaviour. We're both doing better and we're pushing each other and allowing ourselves to be pushed. That's how you get somewhere, don't you see that?"

"Ya but still, it's not so easy to walk the talk. But you're right, except I think you're doing fantastic and me, ya, I'm doing better than I was. But you'll see, I'm going to do much better."

"Look Josh, you've successfully raised a son for eight years and he is a great kid! Me, I chose two selfish bozos to live with; the first one was a loser and the second one was a big shot with a big temper. Neither of them gave a hoot about what I did with my life. Really great choices I made!"

"Those guys weren't good enough for you. You have to realize that you're terrific; you deserve someone who really cares and values you. Anyway, enough about them. It's about now and the future and I have a feeling now that we're exactly where we should be to turn our lives around."

"Wow, look at whose all optimistic and cheerful now!" smiled Monica. At that moment, she had a true sense of gratification. "Here's to giving it our all. Hey, are you up for one more quote?"

"Sure, I love the quotes you shared earlier."

OK, this one is by Maya Angelou as well. She wrote, ***'Success is liking yourself, liking what you do, and liking how you do it'***. I love that 'how you do it' part. I'm going to work on that."

"As am I, starting now. In fact, do you mind if I keep our Journal tonight? I'd like to go over all the points we've made so far and maybe add a few." Monica was happy and relieved to hand over the Journal. To her it meant that Josh was now totally committed or very close to it.

"Good night and thanks for the beautiful evening JJ. You really should be proud of yourself tonight. It takes courage to look at yourself, the real you. I know, I do it all the time and never feel good enough. I want to feel good enough. Whether you know it or not, you're helping me too. You make me feel important. You boost my confidence so that I can say what I think and how I feel."

"That's because you are important and extraordinary. Boy that really was a special night, one of the best ever. No more blaming other people or dragging my feet. From now on, I'm going to like how I work. I want to feel proud of myself. So I have to expect more from myself, do things better, take important things more seriously, learn and be the man I want to be. YES I CAN AND WILL! Monica, you are my muse!"

"And you Josh, you're my anchor. I feel totally safe with you. It was a really special evening. We had fun and got a lot done too! Night."

"Hey Monns, hold up a second. I just realized what my problem has been all along. It's the walk your talk thing. See, I would always say "I KNOW" either inside my head or out loud. And most of the time I did know. But I didn't DO what I knew was right or best, except when it came to raising Bean. Everything else, like my work, my thinking--if someone advised me or if I read something intelligent, I would just think 'I know that' but I never translated that knowledge into any important action. So like service, like when you said the thing about thinking like the Customer and making that Customer feel as if they really matter, I've always known that but I never went out of my way to do anything about it, not in service, not in anything, except Bean. I could talk a good line but I just did everything the easy way. Man, I was such an imbecile! IT'S NOT ABOUT WHAT YOU KNOW. IT'S ABOUT WHAT YOU DO WITH THAT KNOWLEDGE!"

Monica thought for a moment. "Josh, I think you're being pretty hard on yourself but what you just said is true. It's not about what you know; it's about how you use what you know. Most people say 'I know' when they really don't know the half of it.

Josh clasped his hands on the back of his head and stared at the star-studded sky. "I do need to be harder on myself. I want to be the best I can be in everything I do. Otherwise, what's the point of anything?"

Monica understood and responded with an understanding smile. No words were necessary.

That important evening marked the beginning of a new future for Josh and Monica, to the extent that neither could yet imagine.

## Chapter 10

# ***The Zaney Visit***

Josh wanted the next visit to be Monica's choice, since he had no idea yet where he wanted to go for his first escapade. Once Monica decided, she was so excited, she was in orbit. "Hey Josh, I've been thinking about it and know exactly where I'd like to go. I want to buy myself a new face!" What do you think about that? Yes? No?" Josh had no idea what Monica was talking about.

Monica pleaded, "Say yes, please. I'll buy you coffee for a week! Why are you looking at me that way?"

"Because," laughed Josh, "You have a great face! I like your face the way it is. You mean like Botox?"

"Makeup Silly! Botox? No way! Monica laughed uncontrollably while Josh stood there, confused and somewhat embarrassed.

"Oh, I see. How on earth was I supposed to know that's what you meant?"

"Duh, maybe because you have a Sister! What's wrong?" asked Monica. Josh suddenly became quiet, as if he was recalling or thinking about something relevant.

"You know Monica, what happened just now, with our

communication--it really reminds me of Abbott and Costello's *'Who's on First'* sketch! Man, what a classic piece. Now, they were funny. You must have seen it--I mean it's legendary!"

Monica shook her head. "Never heard of it. Of course I've heard of Abbott and Costello but *'Who's on First'*, what's that about? First what? You mean like first base?" Monica was perplexed but intrigued.

"Oh man, you don't know what you're missing! See, a guy named 'Who' was on first base. So Abbott tells Costello that 'Who's on first'. Then Costello yells in frustration, ***'WHO IS ON FIRST'?!*** Abbott keeps trying to tell Costello that the guy on first base is called 'Who'. But Costello doesn't get it. The play on words make the communication really crazy. You have to see it. My Mom has it on video. It is classic miscommunication. That's what hit me when you said you had to get a new face. You have to admit, that's a weird way of saying you're going to buy makeup. Promise me Monns that you'll watch it on U-tube tonight."

"OH! So one guy is asking, who's on first base and the other guy says it's 'Who'? Like, the guy's name on first base is 'Who', right? Monica was really into it. That is funny! So then what happens, in the routine I mean?"

" ***'Who'*** throws the ball to ***'What',***" explains Josh.

"What? JJ, speak English!"

"No, the guy called ***'Who'*** throws the ball to the guy called ***'What'***. See what I mean? It goes on and on like that to show how communication between people can get all mixed up and misconstrued. See, Abbott won't go out of his way to explain what he means. Then Costello feels stupid and gets totally frustrated. It's absurd but it's pure genius! It's been around for almost one-hundred years…not quite but close enough… and I bet it will still be a model of miscommunication in another hundred years."

"I love that!" Monica wrote a few notes, as she refocused her thoughts on their upcoming visit to Zane's Drugstore. She was pretty impressed with Josh's knowledge of the Abbott and Costello routine and made a note to watch it.

"Anyway," resumed Monica, "So I thought we'd go to Zane's, because I heard they have a really nice selection of makeup and, I think it's a good place to test service. Plus, it's something that's completely different from food, right? You still OK with that? I mean if you have another place in mind, we could do the makeup thing another time. And by the way, I like learning about things like the Abbott & Costello routine. But the thing is, that even though it was performed a long time ago, the message is still so relevant, like you were saying. People confuse each other all the time and..."

"You got it. It's fine with me, going to Zane's. I know zero about makeup and I stand by what I said before--you look great now. You don't need all that junk on your face. But if that's what you want, then let's go and get you a new face."

"Men, you're so predictable! I thought you could help me assess the service and the atmosphere in the Drugstore. I, woman of many talents, shall do the makeup part. And by the way, Mr. Cool Guy, it's not a crime for someone of the male species to have some knowledge about makeup you know. We women are expected to know about men's products. Notwithstanding that, it's good to know chauvinism is alive and flourishing. So take that and put it in your ...whatever."

"Really Monica? For your information, Miss-I-wanna-new-face, I sometimes go with Maureen when she's shopping for clothes. ***She*** values my opinion."

"Well, how nice for you both. So, can we go already? I do know you're not a chauvinist JJ...and you'd better not turn into one. I've had my share of that man breed."

The jostling continued on the drive downtown. It was Monica's way of releasing stress and Josh enjoyed the verbal scrapping.

As our two Compatriots arrived at Zane's Drugstore, they almost bumped into a poorly placed pavement sign that read, 'PLEASE USE SIDE DOOR'.

"I hate that!" shouted Monica, as if she wanted everyone around her to know it. If I want to go in this door, then I should be able to. If I hadn't seen the sign, I could have walked right into the glass and I almost tripped over the sign too. Why have a door there if you're not going to use it? Why put a frown on a Customer's face even before they walk in the door! And furthermore, what a thoughtless place to put a sign!"

"You're in a great mood Monns. Actually, you have a point, about access. It's like you always enter a parking lot from a particular place and then they decide to do some repairs on the pavement right in that very place, usually during the busiest part of the day. It's the same kind of annoying thing."

"Exactly!" For once today we agree," Monica replied, breaking a smile.

As they approached the makeup counter, they noticed there were two female employees behind the counter, chatting and giggling. Monica and Josh waited at the counter, a few feet from the employees. Neither of the women were even looking their way, so after a few moments, Josh went for a walk around Zane's to see what was happening in the rest of the Store. It was just after 11am Friday.

Monica deliberately started tapping her fingernails on the counter in an attempt to catch the attention of the two chatty employees. One of them had looked over and signalled to Monica with her index finger that she would be there in a moment. Monica was becoming more annoyed by the minute. She grinded her teeth and took deep breaths and finally called out, "Excuse me, I could use some help over here, please." Monica had been waiting five minutes but it felt like fifteen. She noted in her Journal that five minutes of standing and waiting felt like 'an eternity'.

One of the employees then made her way over to Monica. Her name tag read 'Randi—Beauty Consultant'. The other employee began straightening out some products on a nearby set of shelves. However, Monica thought the shelves looked perfectly fine, which made her wonder who was supervising these people.

"Did you need some help?" asked Randi half-heartedly, ostensibly oblivious to the amount of time that Monica had been waiting and totally insensitive to her obvious displeasure.

Monica kept her cool, remembering that this was all in the name of an Assignment. She began, "Hi Randi, I'm Monica and I really need some new makeup."

"What are you looking for exactly?" Randi asked, chomping on her gum. Monica paused. The gum chewing was both annoying and distracting. Although her impatience was growing, she remained composed as she mentally mourned for the exquisite service they had experienced at Kat's Paradise.

"Randi, I'm looking for makeup products that will bring out my features better, especially my eyes. Gosh, I really don't know... I've been using the same products for several years. I heard that you do makeup consultations. I need advice and I've been looking forward to having a consultation with someone, you know having a professional apply my makeup with some new colours and different products. I just would love to have a new look."

At this point Josh returned from his tour of the Store, shaking his head and rolling his eyes at Monica, while attempting not to disrupt the conversation. Monica was relieved to see him.

"So, how are you Ladies doing?" asked Josh, leaning on the counter.

"Randi was saying that she thinks her Supervisor could help me out."

"Ya, sorry. I haven't been trained on consultations. By the way, you have beautiful eyes!"

"Thank you. That's very sweet. So, Randi, you're new here?" asked Monica, trying to warm up the conversation.

"Well, if you can call three months new--I guess. Hey, do you like Bobbi Brown?"

"Never heard of him," replied Monica.

Randi could not contain her laughter. Oh, no, no--it's a brand of makeup. It's all I use."

Monica and Josh looked at each other and shouted in chorus, "WHO'S ON FIRST!" They both tried fiercely to contain their laughter.

"Excuse me?" declared Randi.

"Nothing, sorry, just an inside joke," replied Monica.

"Bobbi Brown is the only brand I really know. I think I should ask my Supervisor to help you. Usually people know what they want. I'm just a salesgirl still."

With that, Randi left to find her Supervisor. Monica thought it was a little sad that someone had not trained Randi yet. She and Josh then found themselves waiting at the counter again. "This is crazy," muttered Monica. "Too much waiting. If Kat's was paradise, then this is purgatory. So what did you see on your walkabout?"

"I'll tell you later. Not impressed," responded Josh with obvious displeasure.

"Can't wait to hear about it. What's taking that Girl so long! You'd think that if she's been here three months, someone would have trained her by now. And she's wearing a tag that says she's a beauty consultant for heaven's sakes!"

Monica's impatience and frustration were intensifying like a volcano about to erupt.

"Who knows," yawned Josh. "But listen, all our visits can't be great like Kat's was. You learn from the good and the bad ones. It's not that easy to train new people you know. Once I had to train someone and still do my own job. It was a real challenge. Anyway, just think of it as a case study. Be cool and let's just see what unfolds here."

"Will you stop with the 'be cool' stuff! So tell me, Mr. Cool, how can a person do their job if they aren't trained at least sometime within their first month? Someone has to make arrangements for a new employee to be trained. It's just common sense. Don't you think that proper training is an important part of delivering great service? I mean, how can..."

As Monica was about to complete her thought, she saw a tall woman, presumably Randi's Supervisor, walking towards the makeup counter. Monica thought the Supervisor looked more like a Vice-Principal. Her expression was austere and she was carrying a clipboard and binder.

"Sorry to have kept you waiting Miss. I was doing some admin work. Randi tells me you would like a makeup consultation?"

"Yes. I heard that you do them here." Monica was becoming excited again for her consultation.

"I can do a consultation/makeup session for you, at 1pm today." The Supervisor's tone was so officious, as if Monica were booking a dental appointment.

Monica looked at her schedule. "OH shoot! I have a class at 1pm."

"Sorry, I just can't do your consultation now," replied the Supervisor. Late mornings are my admin work time. Would you like to make an appointment?" Monica found the icy tone upsetting as the Supervisor glanced up for only a second. "Hello, I'm here, a real living, breathing, feeling human being!" Monica screamed, in her head.

"Miss?"

"Right. I was thinking of something else. No thank you. Actually I have some things I have to get done to prepare for my one o'clock class. I really don't have much spare time. This was a good time for me and since it's Friday, I assumed there would be no problem. I was so looking forward to having someone show me the best way to put on my makeup. Then I would very likely buy some." Monica was pushing hard to get her way to the point where Josh was a little embarrassed. "To be perfectly honest, I've been all through this with Randi and I would appreciate someone, who knows their products, to help me find the right colours and brands."

"Why not give us a call. My name is Judith and you can call reception. They have my schedule. Or just come in when it's convenient for you and we'll help you choose the right makeup."

"This is a convenient time for me."

"So sorry dear. I wish I could help you now but I'm on a deadline to get this work done."

Realizing that Judith was not going to yield one inch, Monica decided it was futile to continue. "Thanks," said Monica disparagingly. She could hardly contain herself from saying what was really on her mind as she left the counter. However, she had gained the knowledge she needed for the Assignment. Once she was several feet away from the counter, she stopped and made some notes in the Journal.

"Boy, the fresh air sure feels good after that one," inhaled

Monica. "What a witch! 'Dear' indeed! I hate being patronized. Just thinking about her frosty tone of voice makes me shiver. "

"Whoa, Monns, she's not worth getting all upset over. We can come back here after your class. I don't have any classes after 2pm and Bean doesn't get home until after 3:30pm. I don't blame you for being upset. That was pretty awful service and even worse hospitality."

"Let's go to Rascal's JJ. What a waste of time that was but good information on how not to treat a customer…the whole thing was just **so** frustrating and disappointing."

"Ya, but like you said, what a great example of horrible service. Maybe you should have spoken to the head Manager or asked to see the Owner."

"I was too fed up to even think of that. You know what I kept thinking when that woman, Judith, was talking? I kept thinking about what that Manager at Kat's said to me--'We're on your time, not ours'. It's not as if Judith was serving another customer. She and whoever she reports to put paperwork ahead of customers. That's garbage! If a supervisor doesn't care about the Customer, who the heck will? Yup, at Zane's, they seem to be on 'their time' only! There's just no-good reason for that type of treatment. If Kat's was service heaven, this was service hell!"

Josh listened and agreed with just about everything Monica said. A cup of coffee at Rascal's and she'll feel better, he thought.

Back at Zane's, Randi was also feeling disheartened. She followed Judith, who was walking quickly to the back of the store. "Judith, I feel really bad. I mean I should have been able to help that woman. I lost a sale and I really need the commission. I think it would be best for the store if I were properly trained."

"Don't worry about it Randi," replied Judith, in her usual cool and nonchalant manner. "The customer was a student. She probably wouldn't have purchased much. We can't please everyone. It's not your fault. We will train you but there is also a lot you can learn on your own, like the names of all the products and reading the packaging and inserts, to see what the products do. You have to show some initiative too Randi. Don't just sit and wait for us."

As Judith walked away, Randi returned to the makeup counter feeling dejected and frustrated. She stopped by the co-worker she had been chatting with earlier.

"What's wrong Randi?"

"This place," uttered Randi. "Right now I hate it! If Judith doesn't care, why the hell should I

# Chapter 11

## A Spit on You!

Monica and Josh arrived at Rascal's where they sat down to have coffee and a snack.

"Would you like to talk about it now?" Josh asked tentatively.

Monica explained as she sipped on her coffee. "I know that going to Zane's was part of our service Assignment but for me this was special. I've wanted to go there for a consultation for ages but I didn't have the money. Now we have some money, so I figured I could have my consultation and get a few items and pay for some myself…you know….it's just that I feel horribly disappointed. I was looking forward to this so much."

"You don't even need makeup Monica. You look great!"

"You're so sweet but I do have makeup on now, same old stuff. It doesn't seem right that on a Friday, whatever her name was…Judith…would be doing 'admin work'. I mean Customers are more important than that kind of stuff…I don't even think she likes customers let alone value their patronage…"

Josh interrupted, "I can't argue with that but nobody's perfect. Maybe Judith's boss was making her do that admin work now. Sometimes things are not what they seem. Like there was this time when I was working here at Rascal's…"

"Yup, I remember that. You sure looked adorable in that uniform."

"Anyway, no listen Monns, there was this situation with this Customer and I was at the front counter taking orders. It was a Saturday and I had been on my feet for four hours straight without a break. So I asked a manager if I could go for a break and he said yes, go now. So he loaned me his key and I closed down my register. I didn't even think twice about it."

"So, you deserved to have a break," stated Monica.

"Monns, let me finish the story."

"Sorry, go on. I still don't see what this has to do with what happened to me at Zane's."

"You will. Anyway in front of me was a Customer, in my line and before he could place his order with me, I said to him "Sorry sir, this register is closed now." The Guy was really upset and he turned around and started walking out saying he would never come there again. I felt like an idiot. I should have looked up, taken his order and then, if anyone new came into line, explain to them that I would be closing my register but that if they were in a big hurry, I would help them. Otherwise, if they didn't mind, I'd ask them if they would mind going to the next register. There were three other registers open."

"OK, so what happened? Obviously the customer was being unreasonable or he was having a bad day himself," commented Monica supportively.

"What happened was, I ran over to him to apologize; he wouldn't stop and I chased him all the way to his car. But no matter how much I apologized and I even offered him a coupon for some free food on his next visit, he wouldn't have any of it and he drove off. Boy, was he mad!"

"Yes but you tried to fix the situation as soon as you made the mistake. That is a huge difference, HUGE!"

"Yes but my point is that normally I wouldn't do something like that, you know, close down a register in a customer's face. I was tired and having a bad day and I made a mistake. It happens even to people who try hard and are good at what they do. People make mistakes. So maybe while we're sitting here, that Supervisor, Judith or the first lady who helped you, Randi--maybe one or both of them realizes they made a mistake."

"Oh bro, no offence but don't you see the difference between your mistake and what just happened to me at Zane's?" Before Josh had a chance to answer, Monica shook her head in disbelief. "JOSH, YOU TRIED TO FIX YOUR MISTAKE IMMEDIATELY AFTER YOU MADE IT...WHAT DID IT TAKE, TEN SECONDS UNTIL YOU WERE APOLOGIZING AND TRYING TO MAKE IT RIGHT? And look at the lengths you went to, to make it right! Nope, no comparison and I mean NO COMPARISON! C'mon Josh. You and I both know that Randi was, at best, ambivalent and Judith, well, that woman should not be in charge of Employees or be allowed anywhere near a Customer. She reminds me of those insincere, self-important, bureaucratic, arrogant, hollow administrators, like the ones you see in old black and white movies. All they do is give orders and dictate letters. In those days, the most important person in an organization was the boss. In those days, people had more dispensable income. But now, things are different. Businesses and institutions have to care about the customer, if they intend to survive and flourish. No Josh, maybe there's a chance of an excuse for Randi but for Judith - no way. She belongs in the dinosaur age. And I really don't care for young women who pretend to be stupid or play the 'poor me' role. Randi could have made an effort. She didn't seem to have the courage or resourcefulness to even try."

"OKAY, Professor Flowers, your line of reasoning is impressive, not to mention the way those adjectives rolled off your tongue. How about we move on to what we learned from this experience, for our service report?"

"I'm still too angry to be objective. When my Mom gets mad

at someone outside of the family, someone who has offended them, she says 'A spit on them!' That's what I was saying in my head to Miss snotty-faced Judith.

"A spit on them? That's kind of a weird expression Monns."

"My Mom said that her Mother and her Grandmother used to say it--Oops, must go. I have a class and fifteen pages to reread. I mean I've read them but they didn't totally sink in, so I want to read them again. See ya Josh. Thanks so much!

Monica gave Josh a quick hug, then hurried out to catch the bus."

As Josh finished his coffee, he realized how shook up Monica must have been. "Man," he thought, "She didn't even ask me to drive her to school!"

One of the servers came over and asked Josh if he would like his coffee refilled. He declined the offer.

"Have a nice day" said the Server.

"I can't stand that *Have A Nice Day* BS!" muttered Josh after the Server left. Josh wanted to shake off the negative attitude and hostile feelings that had come over him. He sensed that the disappointing visit experienced by Monica, coupled with her subsequent venting, had stimulated his present antagonistic mood. He felt badly that Monica hadn't experienced the kind of service she deserved. He began thinking of ways to make her feel better. As he left Rascal's, Josh continued to mull over what had happened that morning. He then walked towards the exit and mindlessly bumped into the glass door. "Ow, Ouch, Jeezzz!!" he growled, a little embarrassed and ready to give the door a good kick (which he didn't).

Unexpectedly, Josh broke a smile. His head hurt, his nose hurt but all he could think of was, "A spit on you, damn Door!"

Josh wrote in the Journal, ***"BAD VIBES ARE CONTAGIOUS!!!"***

# Chapter 12

## The Autopsy

***"Individual commitment to a group effort—that is what makes a team work, a company work…"***

***Vince Lombardi***

Monica agreed to meet Josh at his place on Saturday to discuss the important points about their disastrous visit to Zane's.

"Hey Bean," as she gave the little Guy a big kiss. "Beany, hope you don't mind your Dad and I working here for a bit on a Saturday. I know that's your special day to do stuff together."

"No, I don't mind," Bean smiled. "I like it when you come over here Monica."

Monica beamed.

"Hi JJ…do you think I could have a glass of water?"

"Water, coming right up."

Secretly Josh loved it when Monica came over. Aside from Josh's Sister, Maureen, (whom he had always called Mau) Josh wasn't really exposed to many women since he had become a Dad. It was a real treat for Josh to see Bean and Monica get along so well. The two seemed so comfortable and cheerful together. Bean treated Monica like an older sister and Monica was more than happy to play the role. She had always adored Bean.

Monica sat on the sofa with Josh watching Bean play with his

Robot toy. She seemed lost in her thoughts.

"Hey, is everything OK, I mean besides the fact that you had a nasty experience at Zane's and not being able to get your makeup and all?" asked Josh with genuine concern.

"I start a part-time job next Sunday, working every Sunday from 8am to 4pm at Rascal's, ironically on Service at the front counter. I need the money and this will give me an extra $300.00 or so each month. I thought, well if I have to work another job, then it might as well be in the area of Service. I thought that the money I get from coaching Lian, Chan and Cheng would be enough, along with what my Mom pays me for helping her out but I'm still behind. I've cut back on expenses as much as I can but it's hopeless."

"Monns, stop for a minute. Listen, do you remember I told you that my Dad's Mom passed away?"

"Yes, I remember. You were pretty upset at the time."

"Well, she left me $5,000.00 in her will. I want to help you out as much as I can, just until you catch up."

"Joshua Johnson, you're the best friend anyone could ask for! Honestly, I did not come here to ask you for money. I'm in dire straits, so I have to accept your generous offer. I didn't know what I was going to do. If I could just borrow say $200.00. I will pay you back, a little each month. I insist on paying you back, with interest."

"No interest Monica. It really is my pleasure to help you out."

Monica felt both relieved and grateful. "Oh you, I adore you," she uttered spontaneously. This was followed by a big smooch on Josh's cheek.

"You mean the world to me Monica." They looked at each other, both speechless, each not knowing how serious the other was about their affectionate comments. They had never spoken to each other quite that way before. The awkward moment triggered a quick change of topic.

"So, shall we get on with this dissection of our adventure at Zane's," stuttered Monica, crossing her legs.

"Sure, let's be objective and just go over the strengths and weaknesses of the whole Service thing there. I just wanted to say, I'm sorry that your visit to Zane's was so disappointing for you."

"Thanks. Let's just move on. It was a good way to learn a few things," stated Monica. "Okay, so I'll just start off here. Well first of all, there was the unfriendly sign to use the other door. That was inconvenient in my opinion and the appearance of the store, just inside the door they asked us to use, was not very attractive. The closed entrance definitely gave you a better overall view of the store. If they're going to change the access, they should at least make sure that the new one is attractive and inviting."

"Secondly," continued Monica, "Randi was not trained. Had she been trained, I would have been able to have a consultation and would likely have purchased quite a bit of makeup. Then Randi wouldn't have had to find Judith and all would have worked out well, most likely. And the fact that Randi kept me waiting so long really shows that she didn't care much. Talk about NOT thinking like a Customer! Time goes so slowly when you're standing and waiting."

"Thirdly, Judith didn't behave as if the Customer's satisfaction was her top priority. She was more concerned with her own priorities. Let's assume that Judith did have a deadline to get her admin work done. I would assume that her boss would have preferred that she make a sale and finish her admin work afterwards. If that's not the case, then the boss is an idiot. Whatever the reason, something is definitely wrong there."

"Final point, Judith was a cold fish. She was so officious ... my way or the highway kind of attitude and stern tone to match. And poor Randi probably felt horrible afterwards. I know I would have felt really stupid if I hadn't been trained and couldn't help a Customer. I'd like to think I would have at least tried harder than Randi did. She acted so helpless. She should have made a greater effort. She was really wimpy and acted like a victim. Okay, so she had no training. There must have been someone in that place who knew something about makeup, other than Judith. Or at least Randi could have tried to serve me. She was really immature…keeping me waiting for no good reason and being so helpless. After all, she had been there three months, so you would think she would have tried some of the makeup or at least learned the colours or something for heaven's sakes. I also wonder how hard she tried to get trained, although I'm hoping our visit made her realize that she has to go for it. I also wonder if there was any stereotyping by Judith, like was she thinking 'oh this Customer probably won't spend much because she's a student', which she could tell from your jacket. I wondered about that."

"Yup, I hear you and I agree. The key thing was that the Customer, who happened to be you, was left very unsatisfied for no good reason. Customers have to be the first priority! It just makes sense. Remember the Manager at Kat's when he said ... 'we're on your time, not ours'. Now that Man knew what he was doing. And it didn't come off as a line either. He definitely meant it. His actions were proof of that. It's a mind-set. You either believe the Customer should receive the finest service from you or you don't."

Josh continued, "Also, I asked one of the Staff which eye drops were best for itchy eyes from allergies and he told me to ask the Pharmacist. Why didn't he go and ask the Pharmacist. Anyway, I went and asked one of the Pharmacists and he pointed me towards the eye drop section but he didn't volunteer to come and show me which one he was recommending. It would have taken him one minute to help me out. Bottom line, no one seemed to give a hoot about the customer. I do think Randi cared some but not enough. Like you said, she just didn't have that gusto, to try and make things happen. Oh, and I forgot to tell you, when I was taking that walk around Zane's, I noticed that the two Employees, at the main cash registers, hardly even looked at the Customers when they were putting through their orders. And their tone, holy crap, it was as if they were half-dead...monotone all the way. They didn't even say 'Hi' or anything and then they just put through each item, told the customers the total amount and asked if there would be anything else. Then there was a half-hearted 'Thanks'. One of them didn't even say anything at the end, just packaged up the order and that was it. There was no upbeat vibe anywhere in that place. Actually, the whole Staff seemed lethargic, bored or apathetic. No service mentality there, none... Z E R O! Talk about negative energy! Oh boy, if they only knew how bad that made them all look."

"Wow, that's awful Josh. It makes me feel angry."

Josh started thinking, then pacing. "I'm beginning to see what my Mom meant. I don't remember the situation but she said. "Josh, there are two kinds of people in this world, the Givers and the Takers". Just the other day I heard these three Guys talking in the lounge about how productivity in Canada has gone way down. And you know why? Because there's a mentality of entitlement, that's why, not by everyone mind you."

"Entitled to what?" questioned Monica.

"Entitled to do the bare minimum and get paid the maximum. They think the easy jobs that pay a lot are the best jobs. There's no pride in their work. If they don't like it, well they get an EI headache...that's Employment Insurance, in case you didn't know. Or they try to bring down the place where they're working and make a formal complaint so they can get money. It's all ass-backwards! That's the kind of attitude I saw at Zane's, right up to Judith."

"That's a pretty pessimistic picture Josh. I don't believe everyone's like that. Look at Ashleigh and the other People who worked that night at Kat's. They were not at all like that. Anyway,

I certainly have no desire to go back to the negative, downbeat energy at Zane's. You know, there's this Guy, Jeff, in drive-thru at Antonio's. I love their tacos. Every time I go through there, he makes me feel as if I've made his day. I go about once a week. He makes me feel like I matter and you know what it is Josh, it's his HOSPITALITY—the way he greets me, says my name, asks me how things are going, and before I know it, I have my order. Then he makes me promise to return so, in his words, "he can have another happy day". What a charmer, but not in the way that he's coming on to me. He just makes me feel special, you know? I think that's 80% of the reason I go there. Anyway, about Zane's, there are a few things I left out, like who was keeping the employees busy or watching out to help Customers...NOBODY, that I could see." Josh took a breath.

"Furthermore," he continued, "the Managers, they were straightening Band-Aids on shelves instead of helping Customers and helping at the service line. There were four customers in line and two managers doing everything except helping out with Service. It was pretty bad Monns. It was as if the Managers were hiding from the service line."

"I think next time I'll go to Hair Plus for my makeup consultation. I heard they do great consultations there. Anyway, so what about you Josh, where do you want to go for your first Service assessment?"

"I'm not sure yet. I was just thinking about our responsibility in this situation with Zane's."

"Josh, we were Customers. We don't have a responsibility, except not to break the law and not to be rude."

"Monns, just listen for a minute. Yes, we do have a responsibility, that is, if we really care about Service in our City. Inferior service makes New Plateau look bad. So, if we care about Service and New Plateau, it's up to us to inform someone about your experience at Zane's, someone who can do something about it, like the Owner."

"That's true. I do care about New Plateau's reputation for Service. So you mean like write a letter of complaint to the Owner or a private message on Facebook, if they're on Facebook, or..."

Josh cut in, "Wait, let's put the shoe on the other foot for a minute. What if you were the Owner? How would you like a disgruntled customer to approach the situation after a negative experience?"

"Well, I know that when there's a family situation or a conflict with a friend, I prefer that the person come to me rather than having them tell the world why they're angry with me. So I guess I could find out who owns Zane's and see if I could make an appointment with the Owner. That's an option. Face to face is always best, when it's possible I guess."

"Monica, I really think that is the best option. Give the Owner a chance to learn what happened when he or she wasn't there. Then that person can do something about it. At least give the Owner that opportunity. I really think it's the right thing to do."

"Wow, I was so busy thinking of my own disappointment, I never saw the bigger picture. I am going to do that. I'm going to phone the Owner and set up an appointment."

"That's great!" Josh was really pleased. "Oh cripes! I almost forgot. I need to have my driver's insurance updated. My insurance company is still charging me for high risk but now that I'm thirty, I should be eligible for a lower rate. I have to call them Monday first thing.

"I think we're done for today," smiled Monica, as she prepared to leave.

"Monns, I made notes of all the things you said and added some of my own thoughts. I think we've covered Zane's from top to bottom."

"Thanks so much for the loan JJ. This was a great session. Yup, you're right. I am going to make an appointment with the Owner, explain what happened to me at the Store and then leave it with him or her to fix the situation. As you said, it's the right thing to do. Hope I can find whoever it is."

As Monica was about to leave, Bean shouted, "Hey Moni, I'm sorry they weren't nice to you at that drugstore. Dad said they just didn't think the right way."

"Your Dad was right. You know what, that's the big difference Beany." Monica stopped, then grabbed Josh's arm. "That's it, what Bean just said, that is it! What Bean just said," she repeated, That the People at Zane's didn't think the right way. ***SERVICE IS A MENTALITY!*** You see, at Kat's Restaurant Ashleigh and the others--they were naturally upbeat and constantly looking for ways to make sure each customer was enjoying themselves. That's how they thought. That was their mentality. At Zane's the mentality wasn't focused on Customer Service. Customer Service was just another part of the job, like stocking shelves or doing admin work. Service is a mentality and it's contagious! Good or bad service is contagious! See, if stocking shelves and admin work is equal in value to servicing customers, then service is just another task when it should be prioritized as the prime objective. Hopefully the Owner will respect that point of view and just maybe something good will come from all this. I'll give it a shot."

"You know," said Josh, as he looked at Monica proudly, "By going directly to the Owner, you're kind of helping New Plateau's economy. When a Customer is upset, they usually become silent complainers, telling everyone except for the Owner. That doesn't help the employees of that business. It doesn't help anything or anyone, just like giving bad service doesn't do anyone any good. The pendulum swings both ways."

"Inch by inch Josh, inch by inch, we'll get there! Thanks again! "For Monica, Josh and Bean, it had turned into a very good day.

# Chapter 13

## *The Insurance Company*

When Monday arrived, Josh was anxious to call his insurance company. He hoped that lady luck would be on his side. He felt very positive.

At first he was greeted by an automated voice message. The voicemail began: "You have reached United World Insurance. For service in English, please press one. For service in French, please press two. For service in any other language, please press three." Josh pressed one.

The automated message continued, "Please press one for personal insurance inquiries or information. Press two for business insurance inquiries or information." Josh pressed one.

The message went on: "For car insurance, please press one. For home insurance, please press two. For group insurance or business insurance, press three. Josh pressed one.

"Thank you," came the reply. "One of our representatives will be with you shortly. Please stay on the line. If you do not wish to stay on the line, please leave your name and phone number and a representative will return your call within twenty-four hours. Or visit our website at *www.worldinsuranceforyou.com* for further assistance."

Then there was music in Josh's ear. He waited patiently at first.

"Oh lord, #%&*!" Josh exclaimed as he accidentally knocked down his coffee. The longer Josh waited, the more impatient he became. "This is crap!" he muttered as he waited for a live, human voice.

After several minutes, Josh got his wish....a human voice answered: "Good Morning ... United World Insurance, Lois speaking."

"Yes, my name is Joshua Johnson and I believe my policy for my car insurance comes due next month. I'd like to check if I could get a cheaper rate. Could you or someone else help me out?"

"Do you have your policy number? What did you say your name was?"

"Joshua Johnson."

"Mr. Johnson, I need your policy number. We have three Joshua Johnson's on file."

Josh quickly yanked his insurance card from his wallet.

"Is your middle name 'Nathaniel'?"

"No, my middle name is 'Victor'."

"Right, here we are. Now what can I do for you today, Mr. Victor?"

"It's Johnson. My middle name is Victor. I have my policy number now."

"I have it too Mr. Johnson; my computer found you. How can I help you?"

"As I was saying before, I was wondering if I could get a better rate. You see, I'm thirty years old now and my understanding is that after age twenty-nine, rates go down. When I was eighteen I had a minor car accident and, because of that and my young age at the time, my rates have been very high. But I have not had any type of accident in twelve years. So I'm hoping I'm eligible for cheaper insurance."

"Just one moment, Mr. Johnson, I will transfer you to one of our agents and I will bring him your file."

It wasn't long before Josh was connected to an agent.

"Yes, Ranj Jarek here. How may I help you."

Josh went through the whole story again.

"Oh, I see you're not in my region Mr. Johnson. Let me transfer you to the right agent for your region. You see we divide our clients by region."

"No, no…wait please! I think it would be faster if I just came down there. What are your hours and is there any special time I should come when the right agent is usually there?"

"Most of us are here five days a week from 9 to 5," answered Mr. Jarek. The agent for your region is Maxwell Lucas. Would you like me to transfer you to his line?"

'Sure, I guess," responded Josh, as he became increasingly frustrated.

"Anything else I can help you with Mr. Victor?"

"No thanks. Have a nice day. Oh, I was just wondering…." It was too late…the transfer was already in progress.

Josh was successfully transferred to Max Lucas' line where he was once again greeted by an automated voice message. "Hi, this is Max. I am out of the office for the next two weeks. If this is an emergency, please contact Ranj Jarek, or leave me a message and I will get back to you when I return to the office. Have a good day."

Josh took a deep, controlled breath. "Why is everything so damn complicated?! Unfriekenbelievable!" he muttered. "What a waste of time! I just wanted to have a simple question answered!" Josh ended the call, too angry to continue with the run-around.

All the way to school Josh was thinking how impersonal the world had become and how mechanically people spoke to each other when it came to service. "Have a nice day, have a good day, have a great day" he sang inside his head ... Why not, he thought, "It was so nice of you to visit us" or just a sincere "Thank you very much", with a real smile and some eye contact?! Or how about on the phone if Mr. Ranj Jarek had actually gone out of his way to help ... what has happened to people?! All these thoughts were giving Josh a headache.

# Chapter 14

## *Hypocrisy at Work*

That night Josh phoned Monica to tell her what had happened so far with the insurance company. "Over 20 minutes on the phone and I got nowhere!" Josh could feel the anxiety coming back.

"That's nuts! I'd be pulling my hair out! It's ridiculous having to go through that kind of maze just to find out some simple information. Time for you to change companies, don't you think? Josh, have you ever heard of P.I.C.?"

"That's People's Insurance Company, isn't it? Ya, I've heard of them through their TV ads."

"You know, I did some reception work and filing for them when I was a Temp. They seemed like a very decent company. They're brokers so they do all the legwork for you. I really think you should contact them. You shouldn't have to go through that kind of rigmarole."

"That's a GREAT idea Monica! A broker! The run-around I got was so infuriating; I just gave up with their diabolical voicemail system. I learned that my insurance company's specialty is transferring people to someone else and then the someone else isn't even there. It's companies like them that make a person cynical, distrustful and crazy!"

"I know the feeling. Anyway, forget them. A good insurance broker will choose the best Insurance Company for you, to suit your needs and give you the best price. I really think you'll get less of a run-around and a better rate. It's worth a try, right?"

"For sure! Now who's the genius? Thanks Monica. You're not just my best friend. You're my smartest friend!"

After talking with Monica, Josh felt a dose of hope. As he stared out his kitchen window, he shouted, "Thank you Lord for Monica!"

During the past week, Josh and Monica had not seen each other much. And now with Monica working Sundays, they had even fewer chances to talk things over. There was still plenty of time to complete their service Assignment. However, Monica liked to get things done early and she was feeling a little anxious. She had told Josh on the phone about her concern that the final report could take them a long time to put together, so she wanted to complete their visits a few weeks before it was due.

Josh knew that he needed a little push now and then from Monica. For some reason that even he didn't quite understand, he liked her occasional prodding. It meant to Josh that Monica cared about his success.

Josh was not one to speak out like Monica, although he wished he could be more outspoken. Without knowing it, his opportunity to do just that was approaching. Josh glanced at the new text on his cell. It was a message from Monica. ***"Call me plse. Fired from Rascal's!"*** He read it again. Josh was in shock. How could that be possible? He reflected on the Sunday before where he proudly watched Monica serving people at the front counter. He admired how she stood out on service, to the point where customers were moving to her line. She was everything a company would want. Something was terribly wrong, a misunderstanding perhaps, reflected Josh. He phoned Monica immediately.

"Are you joking? What the hell happened?! You've only been there three Sundays," declared Josh. "What did you mean?"

Monica was trying not to cry as she forced the words out. "Since I took the job, I've had to do my major assignments on Saturdays so I've been burning the midnight oil. I'm supposed to be in for my shift at 8am but I've been up finishing assignments until about 3am and then I can't sleep. So I fall asleep around 5am and then I have trouble getting in before 8:30am. I tried to fix it."

"Hold on, slow down. Just tell me exactly what happened."

"Okay....After my first shift I asked the Store Manager, Brad, if I could start at 8:30 or 9am, and make it a seven hour shift. He said that there was a rush at 8am and that it was more important that I be there at 8am than staying until 4pm. Their policy is if you're late three times, you're fired. At the end of my shift today, he gave me the news. I tried so hard Josh. I've never been fired from a job before. I just feel so humiliated and I really need the money. Sorry to chew your ear off. It's my fault but I just tried so hard. Anyway, enough about my problems. What happened with your insurance policy?"

"Moni, never mind that! You fired! That is the stupidest thing I've ever heard! I watched you last Sunday when you were serving customers at Rascal's. You were fantastic. This is crazy and not right! I mean you don't let one of your best part-time people go because they have a perfectly good reason to be late, especially if they have asked to be scheduled later. This is nuts! Did you explain to Brad about your, you know, your physical problem and your other jobs, coaching the exchange students and helping your Mom at her Store?"

"I thought I could do it but I'm so exhausted, I just can't think now. And no, I didn't tell him. I don't want to make excuses."

"Go have a rest. I'll call you back and DO NOT WORRY! We will figure this out!" Monica thanked Josh for listening and for his support. They agreed to talk later. After the call Josh's face was red. His hands and brow were sweating. He felt compelled to do something. He shouted for Bean, grabbed their jackets and ran out the door with Bean in hand.

"Bean, we're going on a mission. Dad has to try and make something right. Someone was very unfair to Monica. So when I'm talking with the Man at Rascal's, you just wait in the lobby and I'll see if Jennifer can sit with you there before I talk to the Manager. I have a thing or two I want to say to that redneck."

Joshua had been a bystander for the better part of his life. He was a calm, relaxed kind of guy, very likeable and not easily angered. There were many times when Josh had wanted to stand up for himself or someone else but he always took the passive, peaceful approach. He was becoming annoyed and disappointed with himself for not being more courageous.

"Bean, this time your Dad's going to do the right thing."

"What's a redneck Dad?"

"Daddy was upset when he said that word. I'll explain later. Now we have to help Monica."

"What are you going to do Dad? Are you going to punch the guy out?"

"No! Bean, you know better than that. Physical violence is only for emergencies. What I'm going to do is set the record straight. No more questions for now, OK?" Bean took out his hockey cards from the glove compartment and kept himself occupied."

When they arrived at Rascal's, it was about 5pm. Josh was counting on Brad still being there. He found Jennifer and she seemed happy to sit with Bean for a few minutes. Jen asked Moira, the Floor Manager, if she could go on break and sit with Bean. Moira approved.

"Excuse me," said Josh to Moira. "Is Brad around? It's really important that I speak to him."

"Yup, he's downstairs in the Managers' Office. Good Luck."

"What's that supposed to mean?"

"It means I think I know why you're here. I've seen you and Monica together. It's a shame. She was a real star on service and she was a great team player too, always backed up other people, saved my butt a few times. I probably shouldn't be telling you this."

"Moira, thanks, I really appreciate it." Josh flew through the kitchen, ran down the stairs to the Managers' Office and knocked loudly on the door.

Brad was the only one in the office. As he approached the door, he gave Josh the once-over.

"I'm Josh Johnson. Can I talk with you for just a moment?"

Brad was tall and heavyset, early forties, with a protruding stomach, which hung over his pants. He stared at Josh and then said, "I know you; you're that dude Monica Flowers hangs out with. No doubt this visit is about her? Am I right?"

Josh kept it together and nodded as he took a deep breath.

"Have a seat" said Brad.

Josh sat down and as he was going to begin, he happened to see a sign on the wall that read: ***Mission Statement: "SERVICE IS OUR BUSINESS!"***

"That's a great mission statement," began Josh. "I would think that if you believe that statement, you wouldn't have fired Monica." Josh's exterior was calm but inwardly he was seething.

"Look, Josh is it? It really is none of your business. Monica's not a minor. She should be able to speak for herself. The bottom line is that Monica was late three times and that rule applies to everyone ... three times you're out. I didn't want to do it but I had no choice. If I...."

Josh interrupted...."I know, if you break the rule for one person, you have to break it for everyone...right?"

"See, you get it bro. It's nothing personal about Monica. I mean she's a real looker and that's good for business so, you know, she's good for our clientele of people like yourself." Josh took a second to decipher Brad's remark.

"Monica's not black, she's half Italian!" Josh kept his cool but was becoming more livid by the moment.

"Whatever she is, whatever you are, that's none of my business. To each his own. It's a free country and all that. I didn't mean any offence bro."

Josh wanted to get back on track. Who would make this guy a Store Manager? He could barely contain himself. "Brad, as I understand it, after her first shift Monica asked you if she could start a little later and she explained her reason to you. Would you say that is true...bro?"

"Yup." Brad was rocking back and forth in his swivel chair.

"And would you agree that Monica was great on Service, I mean she really had the potential to be a manager one day."

"Yup, could very well be true. I watched her a few times. She was good with people and helped out."

"And would you also agree that having someone serving your customers, who is an excellent performer, is better than having someone who is not, even if the someone who is not that great can start exactly when you want them to? I mean is it better to have a great person from 8:30 or 9am than to have a mediocre employee serve your customers from 8am to 4pm, just because they fit into your time slot? I also happen to know that it's a lot busier from 9am to 10am on Sundays than it is from 8am to 9am. So why would you insist that Monica be there at 8am?"

Brad leaned forward. "Look, I need a person from 8-4 Sundays, not from 8:30am or 9am but from 8am. And besides that Josh, there are a lot of employees here who go to Horizon and they seem to be able to manage a part-time job and be on time. Monica was just doing one shift a week and she couldn't get here on time. Do you see my point?"

Monica does not like to make excuses but the truth is, that she has a condition called Chronic Fatigue Syndrome. Without going into a lot of detail, she needs more sleep and rest than the average student or else the CFS kicks in. She hasn't had an attack in over six months because she knows how to take care of herself. As you saw, Monica is as fast or faster than anyone is. And, for your information, Monica coaches three Chinese Exchange Students which takes up about twelve hours a week of her time, plus she works at her Mom's store every Friday night and does her Mom's books for her. That takes another eight hours a week of her time.

"Okay, but I'm not sure what you're asking for here. If she's too busy or sick, she shouldn't take on a job here. Look, everyone has reasons and excuses and I've heard them all.

"I did not say she was sick. What I said was that she has to manage her health so that she doesn't bring on the fatigue. Monica can do the shift. She just needs Saturday nights to be able to work late on her schoolwork. It's the only block of time she has to do papers and things like that. Surely you can see that her only mistake was thinking she could get in for 8am in the first place. And right after her first shift, she asked you if she could start just a tiny bit later. Between her classes, her schoolwork, coaching the Exchange Students and helping out her Mom, she's already putting in more than sixty hours a week easily. And when she was working here, was she not outstanding or what? Does that sound like a person who makes excuses to you? All I'm asking is, can any of your other Service People start at 8am or leave at 8:30 or 9am?

"Get real bro! I'm not going to inconvenience everyone for one employee!"

"How do you know you would be inconveniencing them if you don't even ask? You know, I used to think this was a really great place. In fact I used to work here before your time. Things sure as heck have changed and not for the better! Since it seems you're not going to change your mind, I just want to ask you one favour?"

"What's that?" asked Brad, twirling a pencil in his right hand.

"I'm asking that you don't put in Monica's file that she was fired. Put something like she wasn't available any longer. Would you at least do that?"

"Yup, I can do that."

Josh told Brad that Bean was waiting in the lobby. Brad put out his hand and Josh reluctantly shook it.

"Glad we could work it out there… Josh."

Josh loped two stairs at a time and rushed back to the lobby. Bean was sitting by himself with his hockey cards spread out.

"Let's get out of here Bean. Sorry I took so long Buddy."

"Can I have a donut Dad?"

"I'll take you to a special place where they have things even better than donuts; they have donuts too but their food is really, I mean, really good! You were such a good boy. I'm so proud of you." Bean grinned from ear to ear.

Josh was very quiet as he drove to Monique's Pastry Shop. He winked at his Son, betting on the cupcakes as Bean's choice. Then he played Bean's favourite CD.

Bean did choose a cupcake with his Dad and they sat together and chatted for a while about hockey and soccer before driving home.

On the way home, Josh picked up the mail while Bean was still licking his fingers. He had not opened the mailbox since Thursday.

Josh had a moment of clarity. He felt good about himself. He remembered something important, an idea that he wanted to share with Monica. Josh hoped it would help to turn things around for her. He was determined that they would finish their degrees, despite the Brad's in the world. He had a feeling that what he had experienced today was a lesson to be learned, that Managers need to have good judgement, know when to be flexible and when to tow the line. That kind of skill, reflected Josh, required more than a Rulebook.

# Chapter 15

## *Managing the Rulebook*

"Dad"...Josh was preoccupied..."DAD!"

"Sorry, ya Bean."

"Tell me what happened. I'm not a baby anymore. I care about Monica."

"No, you're not a baby, not even close," chuckled Josh, as he roughed up Bean's hair affectionately. "See Bean, the Manager at Rascal's let Monica go because she was late for work three times. It's very important to be on time, like it is for school. Monica knows this and so she asked the Manager if she could start her shift a little later because she was staying up late to do her school work."

"You mean Monica got fired? What did the Manager say?" asked Bean, sitting up in a very grown-up manner.

"The Manager said 'no' to Monica. It gets a little complicated."

"Dad, what would you do if you were the Manager?"

"What would I do? Bean, that's an excellent question! It's always easier to think what the someone else should have done." Josh reflected for a moment. "Well, I'd like to think that if the Employee was excellent in all other ways, like Monica is, I would speak to the other People who work on Sunday morning, to see if anyone was willing to change their shift, just a little bit, so Monica could stay. Then, if that worked out, I would explain to Monica that she could not be late again without asking in advance for permission."

"That's a good idea Dad. Why didn't the Manager do that?"

"It's not that easy to change a schedule Bean. You move one person, then that means you have to move another person. But I'd like to think that I would at least TRY to fix the situation. I think the other Employees really like Monica and they want a solution. But like I said, It's a lot of work for the Manager, to talk to each person, then change the schedule and do his other work too."

"I think the Manager should have tried. You're smart Dad. You would make a very good manager. What you just told me reminds me of something really embarrassing that happened to me in grade one, because my Teacher was so stubborn."

Josh knew what had happened to Bean, since the Teacher, Miss Munroe, had told him. However, he pretended not to know, for Bean's sake.

"What happened to you in grade one?"

Bean looked downward as he began to tell Josh about the incident. "When Miss Munroe was talking, she didn't like to be interrupted. I really had to go to the bathroom so I put up my hand. She asked me to put down my hand and said I should wait until she was finished talking. I think she thought I had a question. So I put my hand down. But I really, REALLY had to go Dad! So I put up my hand again and waved my arm in the air, so she could see it was important. Miss Munroe ignored me and gave me a warning look. I couldn't hold it so it came out all over my seat and the floor too. Everyone started laughing their heads off. It was the worst day of my life Daddy."

Josh could see Bean's feeling of shame. "It wasn't your fault Bean. The Teacher should have realized that it must have been very important when you waved your arm. You were very young and in a really difficult situation. Miss Munroe should have known that you would not have waved raised your hand again, unless it was very important to you. I think it was her first year teaching grade one, so she didn't have the experience to handle the situation better."

"Ya, but it was my fault too. I should have gone to the bathroom earlier. I knew I had to go, before I went into class. I was just too lazy and thought I could wait. But it sure would have been way better if Miss Munroe had realized that it was an emergency."

"That's right," replied Josh. "You were and still are a very good student. Your Teacher should have asked you what you needed the second time you put up your hand. She should have been more flexible and caring, even though you had made mistake by not going to the washroom before class."

"Like the Manager who should have tried harder for Monica? That's why I told you the story Daddy."

"Like that Beany. Sometimes people…managers, employers, teachers, students …they don't try hard enough because they don't think they should have to. But if they did try harder to fix some situations, it could make things better. I'm very proud of you Bean. You're a brave person."

---

Josh found himself considering all sides of the issue. Just as Bean should have gone to the bathroom before class, Monica probably should never have taken such an early shift in the first place. But Bean was a little kid and Monica was a mature woman. She didn't think it through. On the other hand, he thought, Brad had been far too stubborn and lazy to explore some options, and as a Manager, he should have tried to make things work out. If no one wanted to change his or her shift, well at least Brad would have made the effort, not only for Monica's sake but also for the sake of the business. Who wouldn't want to have a happy, hospitable employee, like Monica, serving customers every Sunday? Wouldn't it have been worth the trouble, as long as she wasn't late again? These were the judgments and views traveling through Josh's mind, where a solution to Monica's predicament was also brewing.

# Chapter 16

## The Pendulum Swings

***"The greatest discovery of all time is that a person can change his future by merely changing his attitude."***

***Oprah Winfrey***

Josh was about to phone Monica when he felt the urge to quickly thumb through the mail. There was something from People's Insurance Company, the insurance broker Monica had recommended.

Reluctantly Josh opened the envelope. The letter from PIC read as follows:

*Dear Mr. Johnson,*

*Thank you for contacting us. It is always a pleasure to receive a request from a new Client like yourself.*

*We have reviewed your insurance records, along with all of the other pertinent information. We assume that you are still driving the same vehicle as shown on your registration. If that has changed, please let us know.*

*Assuming there are no changes, we have good news for you regarding your insurance premium, which we would like to handle through H.O.I.C., "Hands-On Insurance Company". We have had nothing but rave reviews from our Clients regarding Hands-On. This is a company whose name reflects the kind of service you can expect.*

*Please review the attached information, which displays the amount of your new premium. As you can see, it is $175.00 less annually than the amount you were paying before, with a better deductible offer as well.*

*I hope to hear from you before the end of this month. For your convenience I have enclosed my business card. Should you have any questions, feel free to call, email or fax me between 9am to 5pm Monday to Friday.*

*Once you give your approval, we will look after initiating your new policy.*

*Sincerely,*
*Jeremy Vincent*
*Senior Manager*
*New Clients Division*

"Unbelievable!" shouted Josh--"Bean, Daddy found a good company who's going to help us protect our car." Josh was so relieved. Then he remembered Monica.

After settling down, Josh phoned Monica to see how she was doing. He hoped his new plan would make her feel better but he had no idea what she would say about it. Whatever she was going through, he wanted to help her. She had become a huge part of the tapestry of his life. Josh and Monica against the bad guys--that is how Josh pictured it.

"Hey there, it's me. How goes it Sweety?"

"Oh, just thinking about different ways to get back at Brad...I know, I know...negative energy and all that."

"Monns, listen. I went to see him."

"WHAT! YOU WENT TO SEE BRAD! Why didn't you tell me? That's just great Josh. Now he's going to think I'm some wimpy woman who needs a man to solve her problems."

"No, it wasn't like that at all." Monns, please listen. I went because I wanted to show him what a hypocrite and butthead he is. What with his mission statement and what he did to you--probably the best service person he ever hired--I was as upset as you were. I couldn't help myself."

Monica paused for a minute. "I understand. I just feel so lousy. I appreciate your good intentions JJ. I'll never go back there!"

"I wasn't trying to get you your job back. In fact, you're too good to have a jerk like that bossing you around. He's stupid! I just had to point out to that bozo, face-to-face, that he could have handled the situation differently—way differently!" Josh then shared the whole story with Monica.

"Well, at least it won't be on my record that I was fired. Josh, I really appreciate how you stood up for me. Sorry I got so mad. I know that confrontation is not your thing and...."

Josh interjected, "The odd thing was that going to see Brad and standing up to him wasn't hard. In fact, it was quite satisfying. I finally stood up and did something!"

Josh continued, "Listen, before you say anything, hear me out on this. I have a plan that would mean you wouldn't have to take on another part-time job. I saw this place, a duplex and the top floor is for rent. Anyway, I phoned the people who own it and they sounded kind of desperate. They live in the lower half. They want to stay there because they had it all refurbished and the lower half is bigger."

"What are you talking about?" Monica was confused and a little scared.

"Just listen Moni - give me a chance to explain. I asked them what they were asking for the rent. OK, are you ready? They want $1000.00 per month and that doesn't include the heat but it does include electrical and water. You and I both have cell phones so we don't need a landline. The only extra cost on top of the rent would be heat. What do you think?"

"Whoa! You're saying that we should move in together?"

"No, I'm saying we could save a bundle of money if we both lived in the same place, separate bedrooms of course. Look, together we'd be saving about $400.00 per month. It makes good sense."

Monica was beginning to see the big picture. "How big is it? Have you seen the place?"

"No, not exactly but I did ask some questions about it and got some of the essential info. I really think it would be worth going to see it." Josh was hopeful. There was a pause.

Monica was beginning to get excited. Her goose bumps had vanished. After all, she and Josh had a proven record of many years of getting along plus she and Bean adored each other. "So what did you find out about it, Mr. Real Estate?"

"Okay, it's about 1,150 square feet total. It has one big bedroom and one smaller bedroom, plus it has one full bathroom and another three-quarter bathroom. I thought that was a real positive. It has a kitchen, which already has stools at the counter for eating. That's the only furniture in the place. It has a good size living room and a dining room where I can put my Gram Maya's table--it's in storage now. Anyway, off the kitchen is another entrance and there's a washer/dryer in there. It doesn't have a dishwasher but mine is mobile. It comes with a nice fridge and an older stove, and you and I both have microwaves. Pretty cool, eh? I went online and saw pictures of it. Oh, and the lady said it has a cozy living room too. So what else do we need?"

Josh went on to explain the great location--close to Bean's school, just under a mile from Horizon, one block from a nice park, and there was a grocery store about two blocks away.

"Did you say two bedrooms Josh? How's that going to work?"

"Just fine because Bean has always wanted bunk beds so I thought that he and I would take the large bedroom and the other bedroom would be all yours, as well as the full bathroom. Bean and I, we'd take the other bathroom."

"Josh, are you sure this is what you want to do?"

"Yes Monica, very sure. I've been thinking about this plan for a while but just couldn't find the right place. I really think this could be it."

Monica found herself thinking seriously about the benefits of Josh's proposal. She wondered if she would miss her privacy or if the whole thing would feel awkward. On the other hand she thought, there were so many times when she felt really alone. It was a lot to take in at once, so she decided to withhold judgement and go with Josh to see the duplex. She wondered if he was doing all this for her. Regardless of the reason, Monica felt grateful to have someone who cared about her situation. That night she didn't get much sleep. The idea felt even more appealing by morning. She found herself hoping this would work out.

The next evening Josh and Monica went to see the duplex with Bean. After very little discussion, it was a done deal. They each loved the set-up and the location. They would move in at the end of the month.

# Chapter 17

## *The Eye-Opener*

"Josh, what you did for me, giving up your privacy, looking for a place...I don't know how to repay you. Here's a big hug. Josh reciprocated with a few comfort pats on Monica's back, and then put his hands on her hair by her ears. "I'm doing this as much for Bean and me as I am for you. It's perfect for all of us. You're pitching in with the rent, so you see; you're helping us too. It's good all-around Sweety."

Monica was so grateful. Her Italian heritage and the fact that she was raised as a Catholic led her privately to say a prayer of thanks. She remembered the words of Pope Francis: ***"True Power is Service"***. Maybe the quote didn't fit her situation exactly but she felt that Josh had put a whole new meaning to the word 'friendship'. He had the power and he made it happen. That's a type of service alright, she reflected.

In her Journal, Monica wrote:

> *"Service has power, positive power, to make good things happen."*

Monica was so thrilled that she phoned her Mom and told her the whole story.

Her Mother had always thought highly of Josh.

"Mom, it took all this time and what Josh did for me, all this time, just to realize that service belongs in all parts of our lives. It's a kind of kismet, because Josh and I are taking this course on Service and Hospitality and we're doing field research to check out service in different establishments. And then Josh goes and does this wonderful thing for me. Service is important everywhere, you know what I mean Mama?"

"Service is no easy task," replied Monica's Mother with resolve. "I like that you are taking a course about it. Mia Monica, I know Joshua will take good care of you. I didn't like you living all by yourself and those other boys, they were not for you. I trust Joshua not to take advantage. He is a good man. I'm so happy for you Mia."

As the Owner of a successful Gift Shop, Monica's Mother, Anna, knew a great deal about service and hospitality. ***"You know Mia, very good service takes patience and a love for what you do, even on those days when you don't love it so much."***

Anna had a way of explaining things in plain words to her Daughter, but with compassion and understanding. Or at least, that is how it felt to Monica.

For Monica the key point made by her Mother was the phrase, 'Even on those days when you don't love it so much'. Monica understood exactly what her Mother meant—those trying days when you really don't feel like giving everything you've got to something or someone. Those days, reflected Monica, are the true test of a person's character.

She looked at herself in the mirror and whispered to her image, as if it were a promise, "When life gets all jumbled up, I want to be a better Monica." It was very much a part of Monica's makeup to be introspective. She often stopped to examine her own opinions and behaviour.

# Chapter 18

## *An Unconventional Idea*

Monica checked in with Josh to confirm that he wanted to include the car insurance event in their Presentation. They both thought it was a good idea. As they chatted about their courses at breakfast, they laughed about their initial notion that the Service and Hospitality Course would be an easy credit.

Monica talked about how she always managed to choose the tough courses, like the Women in Business course. "I never heard of most of these women. Can you imagine that? It would be like you not knowing who MLK is! Maybe one day they'll be studying me... Monica J. Flowers, an unsung heroine well ahead of her time," she mused whimsically.

Josh was amused. "Earth calling Monica....you never know and it wouldn't surprise me either. Getting back to reality, I need your help to decide where to go for my first Service visit. At first I thought about buying a jacket but that just doesn't ring my bell. I want to do something different, something unusual, something really challenging. Can we meet in the Cafeteria at noon and talk about it?" Monica happily agreed. She had an idea.

Josh arrived first at the Cafeteria and waited for Monica. When she arrived, she was bursting with excitement. "Josh, I have an idea for you," she whispered while grabbing a tray. "Actually, I was thinking of this for my next visit but then, when I really thought about it, I just knew it was really meant for you. I'll tell you the rest once we sit down."

The Twosome found a table and set down their trays. "Okay, I'm all ears. Are you going to tell me or do I have to guess?

"I'll tell you but don't say anything until I've finished explaining. You said you wanted something different and challenging. This is both of those things. Trust me, this is not something anyone else will think of. I'm sure of it." Monica was gathering her thoughts.

"What is it? You're killing me here with the suspense!"

"Okay, well, you know that Assignment in our Marketing and Ad course. We're supposed to come up with ideas on how to build tourism in New Plateau. But in order to do that, we should find out what the Tourism Department is doing to build tourism." Monica paused for a few bites.

"What's that have to do with Hospitality and Service?" Josh was wary of where this idea was going. "I don't see how..."

"Joshua...LISTEN! Don't you see, we're citizens and people in government are supposed to be working on our behalf and The Department of Tourism is supposed to be building tourism so our City will thrive. So, it would be interesting to see how they deal with us, if we could get a meeting with one of the Managers or Directors in that Department. We could measure things like how generous they are with their time, what information they share with us, if they behave like robots...like remember that time you went to get your driver's licence renewed last year and you told me you might as well have been served by a robot? Do you see what I'm saying? We could assess all kinds of things related to service and hospitality. What do you think?"

"I think you're a crazy woman sometimes...crazy like a fox... but a very smart fox. It is kind of out there. On the other hand, it's diabolically innovative! Well, I said I wanted a challenge and something different. And tourism is something I care about too. It's also important for both our families. You know what? I like your crazy idea. Let's see…'To Get A Glimpse Of How Our Government Serves Us'….yup, I actually love it Monns."

"Just to make sure,  I'm going to run it by the Professor tomorrow, so we can be certain he's okay with the idea, you know, that it's within the realm of what he intended for the project." Just before leaving the Cafeteria, Monica made a note to see Professor Sydney.

The next day Monica met with the Professor. His response was what she and Josh had hoped for. "Miss Flowers, I think that is a…um, yes…it is a unique idea. I wish you and Mr. Johnson the best of luck with it, yes, indeed, the best of luck with that one," he chuckled devilishly.

"Thank you Professor."

Monica texted Josh-- "prof said yes."

# Chapter 19

## Meet Herman Tate

***"Be Careful the environment you choose for it will shape you; be careful the friends you choose for you will become like them."***

***W. Clement Stone***

Josh phoned the Department of Tourism to track down who would be the best person to meet with.

While waiting on hold, Josh noticed that Bean was spending more and more time with Monica. This was freeing up Josh to do a lot of minor renovations in their new home, in addition to allowing him to stay on top of his studies.

Josh finally heard a male voice answer the phone. "Tate here."

Josh had been referred to a Mr. Herman Tate. Apparently, Mr. Tate was the Director of Communications for the Department of Tourism. This connection sounded promising to Josh.

"Yes, I am a mature student at Horizon, Mr. Tate, and not only do I have an Assignment pertaining to tourism in New Plateau but I am also very interested in the field."

Josh succeeded in making an appointment with Herman Tate for 3pm Friday afternoon. When he and Monica arrived at the Department of Tourism, the Receptionist asked them to have a seat.

"Josh, did you prepare questions?" Monica asked nervously. Lord, I hope this isn't too boring."

"Boring? Tourism isn't boring Monica."

But Josh was nervous too. He was mentally going over the questions he would ask. Monica sensed his nervousness.

"I didn't realize it before," she whispered to Josh, "but I'm..." and then there he was, standing in front of them...Herman Tate.

"Mr. Johnson? I'm Herman Tate."

They shook hands and Josh was so surprised that before him stood a black man, he forgot to introduce Monica. As they walked behind Mr. Tate to his office, Josh felt both a sense of well-being and pride that someone like himself held a high-level position in government. Herman Tate didn't waste any time as he began. "Is this lovely lady your wife?"

"I wish!" chuckled Josh. Sorry Sir, this is Monica Flowers, my Colleague. We're working on this together."

"A pleasure Miss Flowers."

Monica shook hands and said how much she and Josh were looking forward to this meeting.

Mr. Tate stumbled a bit as he began; "Very good. So, It was my understanding that you wanted some information regarding what is going on with Tourism in New Plateau?"

"Yes, very much so," responded Josh.

"So, Mr. Johnson, I have prepared a file for you. It contains all of the pertinent information--magazines that we circulate globally about New Plateau, brochures about our tourist sites, which we also mail out and distribute to all of our tourist sites, as well as to our RV parks, hotels and the like. I have included a summary of our Tourism strategy as well." Herman Tate was proud of the information he had gathered for his guests.

"A summary of your tourism strategy?" asked Josh, looking somewhat puzzled.

"Yes, you know, the Planning Phase, followed by the next stage and the next ...how we develop a strategy. I thought that as a college student you might find that informative, perhaps even useful in your own pursuits."

"Mr. Tate, I really do appreciate that but we have lived in New Plateau most of our lives, so although I greatly appreciate your putting together this file of information, we were hoping to find out what is new in tourism here, how tourism will be built further in New Plateau."

"Well, Josh....may I call you Josh?"

"Of course."

"Yes, well Josh, as you know we have focused on pursuing both the Downhill Ski market and the Rock Climbing market and we continue to do that. This year we have visited and met with both government and private individuals from China, Japan, South Korea, Australia, Germany, France, Netherlands and of course a multitude of North American officials as well. We do this to build what is already a relatively strong magnet for our City--our skiing and rock-climbing--which are second to none in North America."

"Yes, that is really great, really great. If you don't mind me asking Sir, if our skiing and rock-climbing are being promoted so vigorously and if they are second to none in North America, then why aren't there tens of thousands of people coming here for those activities?" questioned Josh.

"If I may continue please Josh... and I do appreciate your passion...don't get me wrong...it's very refreshing."

It appeared that Mr. Tate was becoming a little agitated, which prompted Monica to give Josh a swift but gentle kick under the table. She was also having trouble smothering a yawn.

"I'm sure you're working very hard to promote New Plateau Mr. Tate," smiled Monica, still nudging Josh with her foot.

Herman Tate continued. "You see, we can't just get an idea and go do it. We are directed by our elected officials. Then we also have to get a buy-in from the Municipality and then we have to figure out how to finance any ventures. So you see, it's not just about what we think is a good idea but it is also very much about what investors want to invest in. That often determines our direction. Furthermore, we don't have accommodations for tens of thousands of people. These things take time and planning."

Josh was becoming anxious and annoyed with Mr. Tate's guarded response. The voice in his head was saying, "Typical government speak…tell me something I don't know."

"Yes of course, I understand," acknowledged Josh politely… "Mr. Tate, has there been any talk about the ideas which were tossed around a few years ago….you know, having a large marketplace and indoor/outdoor flea market? Have those or any other ideas been discussed or perhaps in the planning process? Or what about the new mall that was supposed to be built near the primary hill?" Josh was hesitant to ask but too curious not to make the effort.

"Not really anything new there, not to the best of my knowledge," answered Tate. "You should run for elected office Josh! I'm not sure there is anything more I can add to what I have already told you. We continue to focus on those activities, which I mentioned earlier. As they grow, so will the accommodation for our guests. A few hotel chains are very interested in coming here. All these things take time. Listen Josh, if you have any more questions, you can always give me a quick call. Rest assured that I am as eager as you are to continue to build tourism here."

Josh thought how limited the Man sitting in front of him was, limited in the amount of change he could or would bring about, limited by years of promoting the existing state of affairs, the status quo. For a moment, he felt sorry for Herman Tate.

"Yes, just one more question, if I may, Mr. Tate?" Josh was a little nervous about this question but thought it was important. His initial expectations of some exciting news had already been dampened. "Um, since you are the Director of Communications, is the Tourism website for our City part of your Department?"

"Yes it is. Jack Hawkins, our IT Supervisor, looks after that."

"Are you pleased with the website?" questioned Josh. I mean do you have any plans to add to it or make changes, adding new photographs, things like that? I'm asking you this because, frankly Sir, I thought the website was rather, shall I say, underwhelming." Monica was stunned by Josh's candour but maintained a calm exterior. Oh, how she wanted a glass of water, or better still, a cup of coffee.

"I see," replied Herman Tate, somewhat taken aback by Josh's frankness. "Well, as you must know, websites are very much a work in progress. I'm in my mid-fifties and have never really acquired a taste for that kind of thing. My wife keeps telling me that I don't know what I'm missing. Quite honestly, we have not received any complaints about our website, so that tells me it's doing just fine. Jack and I do meet occasionally and he updates me. I trust Jack. He has been with us since the website was initiated. Quite frankly, I just do not have the time to watch over our website. As you will learn one day Josh, you have to trust your Staff and I do trust Jack. I will take another look at it with him at our next meeting. Having said that, I believe our Department is one of the best," stated Tate rather defensively.

Mr. Tate began to stand, seemingly signalling that the meeting was over.

Josh and Monica politely thanked the Director for his time and for the file of information. He wished them good luck with their project and they parted with cordial handshakes.

Once they left Mr. Tate's office, Josh was quietly mulling over the meeting. He stopped once or twice to jot down a few notes and then looked at Monica as she silently mouthed the word 'b o r i n g'.

"Coffee time?" Monica asked, as she finally was able to fully exorcise her yawn.

"Yup, just a sec…man, that was an eye opener! I feel kind of stressed. I mean when the Guy first came out to meet us, I felt really comfortable and proud … you know, him being black and all. But then, the whole conversation sounded so typical to me … so predictable and bureaucratic. How can our City grow when the people who are running it don't want to grow? There was no excitement. Josh imitated Mr. Tate's voice, "Well, you know, we've done this and it's not so easy to be innovative…"

"Maybe you're being a little hard on the Guy," Monica commented while chuckling at Josh's imitative performance. "I think Mr. Tate did his best to give us any information he could. But I will say this; to me it's important when it comes to guests, to cross that finish line with grace, and he did just the opposite. He just stood up, out of the blue…like, 'OK I'm done now'…not a savvy way to end a meeting. It felt really awkward. What were you hoping to hear?"

"I would just like to have heard something like, 'Yes! We've got some great ideas in the works'…something like that…anything at all, except for the same old drivel. Someone in that position should be excited about what's coming. The Director of Tourism should be the kind of person who energizes other people, not someone who puts them to sleep."

# Chapter 20

## The Lynching

***"I've learned that people will forget what you said, people will forget what you did, but people will never forget how you made them feel."***

***Dr. Maya Angelou***

Monica tried to tease Josh out of his growly mood as they sipped on their coffee at the Coffee Parlour.

"OK, let's hear it ; what's on your mind? Are you disappointed?"

"I'm more like shocked. I mean, Monica, my Dad is in his late fifties and he's all over the internet. How can you be the Director of Communication these days and not be Internet savvy? It doesn't make any sense! No time to oversee their website? Can you believe that? Do you know that the first thing most people check out is a website when they are looking for information or deciding where they are going to vacation? The guy's a dinosaur!"

Monica empathized. "How about if we start at the beginning." Remember, she said gently, "We were there mostly to assess SERVICE. Yes, we hoped to get some information for our Ad/ Marketing course and we did get... well ... at least some information from all the brochures Tate gave us. I've heard that people like and respect Herman Tate. We were pretty fortunate to have an appointment with him. I'm just saying. But you're right about the website issue.... that was a shocker!"

Monica was bothered by what Herman Tate had said during

their meeting as well as what he had not said - nothing new in the offing; that really concerned her. However, her drive to do well on the project was now her primary goal. Among all of her courses, this project was her biggest concern at this point. She found herself feeling totally fixated on it.

The twosome sipped on their coffees quietly while doing some people watching to help them unwind.

"Here's the thing," began Josh. "It's not as if you and I don't know anything about service or about the economy in New Plateau. You've worked for your Mom in her Shop for years and you've watched her business grow. And my Dad has been working on the Ski Hills half his life and he says they have let people go. Mind you, he does love the extra overtime. My Mom still knits scarves for the Ski Hill but I haven't heard her say business is booming. And your Dad keeps saying he has to let teachers go to meet the City's budget requirements. Being a Principal must drive him crazy, having to tell good teachers that they no longer have a job. And he's even working two jobs if you count his carpentry projects. Even my Sister says that her rock climbing tours have not gone up or down in the past few years. SO, WHAT'S ALL OF THIS PROMOTING DOING FOR NEW PLATEAU? I'LL TELL YOU WHAT IT'S DOING; IT'S JUST MAINTAINING THE STATUS QUO!"

Before Monica could get a word in, Josh was determined to get it all off his chest. He was just getting started.

"Furthermore, our Parents are so busy, they don't even have time to babysit Bean! Like they'll be working until they're seventy-five or eighty at this rate. I think about all these things and then I know--people like Herman Tate just don't get it! We need different strategies and some new attractions and from what I've read in the newspapers, the money is there to develop those things if those old fossils would just get off their butts and open their eyes!"

"I get it Josh. I'm angry about it too." Monica realized the link between the economy and tourism did require her to become more serious about this.

"JJ, I've been so involved in myself and in my own head, I just didn't put it all together....you're so right! It's truly a critical matter."

"Now you see. Why don't they see! Remember when you told me how helpful your Mom was when you were talking with her on the phone about service?"

"For sure I remember. She made me feel so good."

"Exactly! See that is the point of great service too Monica!"

Josh was writing and speaking at the same time:

"TO MAKE THE CUSTOMER FEEL GREAT, THE PERSON SERVING UP THE INFORMATION HAS TO UNDERSTAND WHAT THE GUEST NEEDS AND WANTS, IF THEY GIVE A HOOT! THEY HAVE TO CONNECT! MAYBE THEY'D LEARN SOMETHING IF THEY LISTENED INSTEAD OF DEFENDING WHAT THEY'RE DOING! THEY BECOME TOO COMFORTABLE AND CAN'T BE BOTHERED TO THINK ABOUT WHAT THEY COULD DO BETTER. *SAME OLD CRAP PRODUCES INERTIA!*"

Monica marvelled at how incisive Josh could be. He really knew how to make a point relevant.

"What simple concepts JJ, to make the person you're meeting with feel like they matter, to actually listen, maybe even change direction, because you heard something that could stimulate progress. Hey, let's make a list of the Strengths and Weaknesses regarding Herman Tate's meeting with us. We're really getting somewhere here."

"Monns, you always have the common-sense approach. Sure, why don't you take the lead on the Strengths element. I'm dying to hear that part."

Monica wrote the following in their Journal.

***Strengths of Service & Hospitality by Herman Tate***

1. *HELPFUL ... He prepared a file of information for us in advance.*
2. *COURTEOUS ... He came out of his office to greet us.*
3. *ACCOMMODATING... .He met with us 3 days after JJ's phone call.*

"Monica, do you mind if I say something about those three strengths?"

"What? They're each true."

"First of all, let's look at COURTESY. Yes, that was a nice gesture when he came out of his office to greet us, rather than someone pointing us in the right direction. That showed respect for us as guests. But what's the first thing you would do once someone was in your office for a meeting?"

"Offer them a seat?"

"After that, what would or should you do?"

"True, I wouldn't have minded some coffee or something," confessed Monica.

"Exactly. At least offer coffee or a glass of water. He had an empty mug sitting right in front of us. Either he didn't think of it, which I doubt, or he didn't want the meeting to be too long. A guy in his position is not stupid or ignorant about meeting etiquette."

Josh continued, "I do agree that the Man was ACCOMMODATING and that it was HELPFUL, even THOUGHTFUL of him to prepare (or maybe he had it prepared by his Assistant)... anyway, he had a file of information for us and that was intended to be helpful. So I'll give him that much."

"OK, Einstein, what do you think the Weaknesses were?

Josh then wrote in their Journal.

***B. Weaknesses of Service by Herman Tate***

**4.** *Didn't LISTEN to what I was saying.*

**5.** *Was defensive.*

**6.** *Didn't ASK Monica for her input.*

**7.** *Didn't have sufficient KNOWLEDGE about their Website.*

**8.** *Didn't show APPRECIATION for our interest in Tourism.*

**9.** *Didn't cross that finish line with Grace (quote Monica!)*

"He listened to your questions," insisted Monica.

"Really, you think so? Let me ask you this. How do you know when someone is really listening to you?" asked Josh confidently.

Monica thought for a moment. "I guess their body language and eye contact, things like that."

"Sure, those things are very important but they're just part of it. A few years ago, I took this outstanding course for Managers called 'Listening & Communication', by a Mrs. Joanne Parker. She demonstrated that our level of listening is determined not just by our body language but also by HOW WE RESPOND to what we have heard. So the Guy made eye contact but he didn't really listen...he didn't Monns."

"Give me an example....you've lost me." Monica was very curious as to what Josh was getting at.

"Okay," replied Josh, "This is REALLY IMPORTANT…CRITICAL. If you ask someone a question, by brushing it off, like Herman Tate did, it shows you don't care about the question or respect the person who asked it. If you don't understand a question, then you should ask for clarification, that is, assuming you're interested in the question. For example, you might say, "So what you're saying to me is...." Or, if you do understand the question, you encourage conversation by opening up the subject, not by closing it down like Mr. Tate did when I asked him about the Marketplace and the Indoor/Outdoor complex. What I'm trying to show you is that your Mr. Tate didn't want to listen or understand my point of view. I call that a DISSERVICE to a guest. Then when it came to my question about the Tourism Website, that was even worse. He didn't even care—he just brushed it off. Boy, would I love to get my hands on that website and make it come alive!"

Monica was fascinated. "I never ever realized that! I love what you said about how you can tell if someone is really listening. Imagine all the information we humans could accumulate if we really listened to each other. There's a great quote by Larry King. He said something that I keep reminding myself of when I talk to much... 'I never learned anything by listening to myself talk'. It's so true!"

"You can say that again. Monica, you know it really is great working with you. Maybe I feel that way because you really do listen. You make me feel important. That's how Herman Tate should have made us both feel. But you see, he just goes along, thinking the same way, always careful not to rock the boat. After all, look what he has to lose—a six-digit salary, vacation that grows by the year, benefits galore. And what does he have to gain if he were to choose to rock that boat, to go against the grain, demand and fight for meaningful change? I'll tell you what he would have to gain—more work, standing up for what he believes in and maybe even a transfer to another department or a nice severance package. Would he take the chance that maybe, just maybe, there would be other people of like mind who would join him in creating and fighting for meaningful change, change that could really help New Plateau? Now that would be serving the needs of the people he's supposed to be working for--the Citizens of our City. Guts, these bureaucrats have no intestinal fortitude, not the ones who I've met anyway."

"Wow, that's a whole lot to think about. We do need people who really care, to be in positions like Tate's. We need gutsy leaders. You're absolutely right. One day hopefully you'll be able to make that speech to some movers and shakers. I think you're going to be a real force in this City one day JJ."

Josh was still pretty riled up so Monica continued, this time with a question that had been on her mind. "Josh, do you think we did a good job of listening to Mr. Tate? I mean when he talked about what they were doing to promote New Plateau's ski hills and mountain climbing, we probably could have replied with more enthusiasm. And when he talked about the obstacles to having more tourism projects, like the ones you mentioned, we could have shown more understanding by not putting him on the spot so quickly."

Before Josh could respond, Monica began to answer her own question. "But you know what, I tend to agree with you. WE WERE MR. TATE'S VISITORS, HIS GUESTS AND THAT MEANS THE ONUS WAS ON HIM TO PROVIDE HOSPITALITY. THAT HOSPITALITY SHOULD HAVE INCLUDED ALL THE THINGS YOU JUST TALKED ABOUT. SOMETHING GOOD COULD HAVE COME OUT OF THAT MEETING. HE OBVIOUSLY DIDN'T THINK HE COULD LEARN MUCH FROM US...VERY OLD SCHOOL." Monica wrote it all down.

"It's going to be a challenge when we write up this experience! I'm learning so much my head is spinning. JJ, you OK?"

"Hey Monns, I can't take any more serious talk right now. Are you up for a Games Night? We could buy a couple of new games. I could use a break."

"Great idea. Let's go find some games. Bean is going to love this." Monica's thoughts were still fixed on Josh's explanation of good listening skills. As was her style, she wondered if she had been a good listener to those people she cared about. She resolved to be a better listener.

It occurred to Monica, as they drove to the closest shopping centre, that she had not been out on a date with any men since she had moved in with Josh and Bean. She also realized that she was not missing the dating scene one bit. She chuckled at this realization, as she enjoyed the drive and the landscape.

Game night turned out to be a huge success. By now Monica felt right at home, despite the fact that Josh and Bean did most of the winning and all of the bragging that night.

# Chapter 21

## *Unexpected Happenings*

Four weeks had passed by since Josh and Monica had been given their Hospitality/Service Assignment. Calculating the workload for their other three courses, the Two determined that they had two more weeks to complete the Visit and Purchase portion of their Service Project. This would leave them four weeks to finalize their Service Assignment while still being able to complete their work for their other courses.

Professor Sydney had posted on his Office Door that the Instructions for writing and presenting the Report would be available the following Wednesday.

It was Monica's turn to make the next purchase for the Service Assignment.

"Going for a makeover and some makeup?" asked Josh.

"Nope. I changed my mind. I want to get some new running shoes and start my morning runs again. I was talking to Koko at school and she lives just one block away. We're going to meet at 6am every Monday, Wednesday and Friday mornings and run together starting next Monday."

Josh was reminded of something regarding their monies from the Professor. "You know, the only money we have spent out of our $525.00 allowance is about $150.00 on the Restaurant visit, so you could probably pay for your running shoes outright with the money from the Professor."

"Yay!" clapped Monica. "Just a minute though, what about all the gas money you've spent driving us both around to all these places? It doesn't seem fair, you having to pay for it yourself. I want to contribute."

"No way….NO WAY! If I weren't driving us around, I'd be driving myself around. That's what I do when I want to think. I drive." Monica gave Josh a big hug. "You know, you're really a great guy. Some lucky woman is going to see that one day. And I'll be there to make sure she's the right one for you, like the song by the Jackson 5—'I'll be There'—watching!"

At school Monica caught up with Jocelyn. She and Jocelyn had been friends for many years. What they had in common at the time was that they both had planned to go back to Horizon and here they were, back at university the same year. Jocelyn was also taking the Hospitality course.

"Hey Jocelyn, how's it going? How are you and Koko doing with the Service Assignment?" asked Monica.

"Monica!" You look fantastic, Girl! Hey Koko told me that you Guys are going to be running together."

"Want to join us Jocey ?"

"Thanks but no ... you know I'm a Yoga girl but thanks for asking."

"So how are you doing on the Assignment? Lots of running around, huh?" queried Monica.

"It's coming along. Koko and I are having a little trouble coordinating our schedules but we're working it out. It's alright I guess. And you, I hear you finally moved in with Josh! Wow, what a cutie he is!"

"No, no Jocelyn! It's not like that. I was in a bind financially and Josh got a bigger place, so it just worked out. But we're not together. We're just great friends."

"Ya, well I wish I could find a 'great friend' like the one you have."

"Oh stop...really, it's not like that! Listen, I have to get to class. Maybe we can have coffee later together? By the way, you look pretty great yourself!"

"Thanks ... bye Monica or should I say Mrs. JJ!"

"You're hopeless---love ya--see you later I hope." Monica adored Jocelyn and enjoyed her teasing, even though she pretended not to. It was Jocelyn's way of expressing affection and Monica knew that.

When Monica got home, Josh had left a note that he was called out of class by Bean's school and wrote he would give Monica a call as soon as he knew what was going on. This was supposed to be the afternoon they went shopping for her running shoes. Monica was worried. What could have happened to Beany? She started to pace. Something was really wrong. She could feel it. She tried Josh's cell phone but there was no answer. That in itself was unusual.

"C'mon Josh, call me!" Monica was frantic. She decided to phone the School. She phoned Brentford Elementary and finally located the Woman who had contacted Josh. Bean was at the Kids' Hospital.

Monica called a cab and went straight to Emergency. Finally she found someone who knew that Bernard Johnson (aka Bean)was on the second floor. Once she arrived on the second floor, she ran to the Nurse's desk. "Bean Johnson or Bernard Johnson ...I was told he is here."

"Are you a relative?" asked the Nurse at the desk.

"I live with Bean and his Dad. Please, how is he? What's wrong with him? Can I see him please! My name is Monica Flowers."

"Miss Flowers, I'll let the Patient's Father know you're here."

Monica was beside herself with worry. "My little Beanie, Oh my God! Please let him be OK!" she sobbed softly, muzzling her mouth with her hand, while digging in her purse for a tissue. Then she saw Josh making his way towards her.

"It's okay. Bean is going to be fine," whispered Josh.

"Oh thank God! You look really tired. Are you OK JJ? What happened? Where is he?" Monica drew a huge breath of relief.

"I know, I was scared to death when the school called me," said Josh, as he wrapped his jacket around Monica. "You're freezing! Listen Sweety, it's okay, it's not serious. During gym class they were playing soccer and Bean bumped into this big boy or vice versa....I'm not sure who bumped into whom.... anyway, Bean was unconscious and that's when the school called me," explained Josh, as he rubbed Monica's hands.

"Unconscious?!" Is he still unconscious?" quivered Monica.

"No...he's just kind of groggy. They're checking for any broken bones or injuries. He's having x-rays right now. They'll tell me as soon as they're through doing the x-rays."

"Let's go to the Waiting Room...c'mon...it's going to be OK. He's a strong, resilient kid. He has to be okay...that's all there is to it," Josh uttered convincingly.

"Josh, I've never asked you this," said Monica with great hesitation.

"What is it? You know you can ask me anything."

"I was wondering, I mean it doesn't matter to me but I was just wondering if you ever heard from Sylvie?"

Josh turned to Monica as he began his explanation. "Nope, not since she left to go back to France after giving birth to Bean. I never would have gotten through that first year with a baby if it hadn't been for Maureen. Moving in with Mau, we were both able to stagger our working hours and look after Bean. What a year that was! But if it weren't for Sylvie, there would be no Bean. If anything happened to him, I don't know what I would do."

"If anything were really wrong, they would have come and told you by now, right? asked Monica, still shaking.

Just then a Nurse was standing at the Waiting Room door. "Sorry Mr. Johnson for the wait-- X-ray was a little behind so your Son just went in for his x-rays about five minutes ago."

Josh and Monica both breathed a long, deep sigh of relief. They waited quietly.

Josh began thinking about Bean's estranged Mother. Nine years ago, an exchange student from France, Sylvie Dubois, came to New Plateau as a first year university student. Sylvie and Josh met at a party, held in a beautiful hotel suite at the Richmond Hotel, hosted by some of the rich kids. The Suite had three bedrooms. The chemistry between Josh and Sylvie was immediate. That was the night Bean was conceived.

When Sylvie found out she was pregnant, she told Josh once she was certain. Being Catholic, an abortion was out of the question for her and Josh wanted her to have the baby.

Sylvie completed her first year at Horizon and Bean was born at New Plateau's Mountain Peak Hospital. Sylvie was only eighteen and she had career plans. She had no interest in becoming a mother. Josh was 21 at the time. He knew that becoming a Dad would mean dropping out of Horizon, and that is what he did. Josh didn't know anything about looking after babies. All of his babysitting jobs had been for kids, the youngest having been three years of age.

Sylvie returned to France after giving birth to Bean in July.

That is when Maureen stepped in. Josh moved into Mau's two-bedroom apartment with the Baby and Maureen helped him looked after Bean, who he named after his Grandfather, Bernard Johnson.

Josh and Monica stood up as they saw the Nurse coming towards them. "Mr. Johnson, you can see your Son now. He is out of X-ray. I'll take you to him."

Monica went with Josh--no way she was staying behind.

As they entered the room, there was Bean with a bump the size of a golf ball on his forehead. The Doctor was sitting on the bed and explained to Josh that Bean was going to be fine. However, they wanted to keep him overnight for observation to make sure there was nothing they had missed. There were bumps and bruises but they would heal, explained the Doctor. Monica hugged Josh as they both began to tease the youngster about his man-sized bump. Doctor Janzen asked Bean a few questions like, "Does your head hurt much?" and "Does it hurt anywhere else?"

Dr. Janzen turned to Josh and Monica assuring them that all the X-rays were clear, showing no bones had been broken nor were there haemorrhages of any kind.

The Doctor smiled, "Bean, you're a very brave boy and you will feel good as new very soon, very soon."

"Hey Dad, I'm a REAL jock now, right?"

"That's right Beany," replied Josh proudly, "But don't go making a habit of proving it by breaking your neck." Bean laughed as best he could. He knew Josh and Monica were worried and he wanted to be brave, even though his head was aching.

The Doctor asked Josh to step out in the hallway for a moment. Josh asked Bean if it would be alright if Monica came with him to speak to the Doctor. The Youngster said "No Problem Daddy!" An Orderly then dropped off Bean's supper.

Dr. Janzen then spoke to Josh and Monica. "Your Son is a very special little boy. He never cried once. I've never seen anything like it. Even the Nurses in X-ray told me how brave and polite your Son was. You've got a very special Child there Mr. Johnson."

Josh was full of pride. He stayed at the hospital and slept in the bed beside Bean that night. Monica went home after giving Bean a big hug and kiss. She too was exhausted but so very relieved.

That night it dawned on Monica the relevance of all this to Life. It was something the Doctor had said that really made her see what was important.

Monica wanted to wait for the right time to share this revelation with Josh. Right now, she just wanted to be with Bean. The Doctor had suggested that Bean stay home from school the next day. Josh phoned Mau to tell her about Bean. Maureen offered to look after her Nephew but both Josh and Monica really wanted to stay with the brave little Man the entire day.

Josh and Bean were home from the hospital by lunchtime and Josh carried him to his room. Monica gave Bean a big hug and several kisses, then tucked him in and brought him a peanut butter and jelly sandwich with some weak tea, just the way he liked it...loaded with milk and sugar. Bean joked that he should get bumped in the head more often, so he could get all this attention.

Josh was brewing tea in the kitchen and taking some muffins out of the freezer. He thought aloud: "I'm supposed to be Bean's rock, his anchor but sometimes I think he's the one who gives me strength. If anything had happened to him..." Josh broke down. Monica held him securely.

"Josh, he's a little boy—as long as it's just bruises and a bump on his forehead --this whole thing really opened my eyes. I've been so closed up for the past year. After breaking up with Marty, I told myself I would never feel anything for anyone again. Let's face it, my choice of men…first Roger and then Marty, well, they both turned out to be good-looking, empty-headed, thoughtless losers. So I just closed myself off. You and Bean have changed my life! You, my dearest Friend, are a fantastic Dad and a strong, wonderful man. Don't you ever think otherwise or you'll have this crazy Italian to deal with."

Monica continued as she saw that Josh was beginning to feel better. "The Doctor was right," she said. "Bean is extra special. When I thought something dreadful had happened to him, I went crazy. I feet such love for him. Bean has treated me like a member of the family. He's so warm and kind and helpful. He's smart and mature… he's amazing! Imagine, it took the love of a wonderful little boy and the thought of losing him that made me really feel something again."

Josh put his hand on Monica's shoulder as she grabbed some tissues.

"There's more… I was thinking last night, when you were at the hospital. I want to give these thoughts justice when I explain them to you." Monica paused as she tried to pull herself together. "The Doctor was right Josh. Bean is extra special and what makes him EXTRA special is that he always cares how he makes other people feel, wherever he is. All Bean could think of at the hospital when he saw you was to make you proud of him. That's just Beanie. He's not all caught up in what he wants like so many other kids. So I realized that there was a huge lesson here for Life and believe it or not, also for how people treat each other in their day-to-day lives and in their jobs or whatever. What makes people extra special is how extra special they treat each other…that's service, Josh. That is what it really means. You have to feel it, not just go through the motions. You have to FEEL IT! WHEN YOU DO THAT, YOU'RE NOT JUST PERFORMING GREAT SERVICE FOR OTHER PEOPLE, YOU'RE ALSO DOING SOMETHING SPECIAL FOR YOURSELF."

"You mean because you're doing the best you can?" asked Josh.

"Not just that...because the people you treat extra special, those people will remember you just like that doctor is going to remember Bean-- your eight-year old son-- whose special treatment of me has caused something extraordinary to happen inside me."

"You're really something yourself, you know that! I'm so happy you're here with us Moni."

"Sorry for being so gushy. It's like the tide just came in all at once, you know?"

"It's a good thing Monica, it really is. It's what you needed. You've been pretty brave yourself."

Josh knew this was not only a big breakthrough for Monica but he also knew she was right. Service had everything to do with how people treat each other. These thoughts crisscrossed both Josh and Monica's minds that entire day.

Funny, thought Josh, that such positive thoughts could come out of what could have been a disastrous accident. He felt that this kind of insight was Monica's gift to him. She saw things differently from other people and she could find a lesson even from the worst situation. That was her gift and today her being there had made all the difference for both himself and Bean.

Josh recalled something his Father had told him. It was a famous quote by Mahatma Gandhi but he couldn't remember the precise words but it had to do with what Monica was talking about. He tried desperately to think of the words, then decided to call his Father and ask him. His Dad remembered. "Mahatma Ghandi was a great leader Joshua. What he said was this: ***'The best way to find yourself is to lose yourself in the service of others'***. Why do you ask Josh?"

"Because Dad, I get it now. Thank you."

# Chapter 22

## *The Running Shoe Story*

Josh and Monica had a few course papers to research and so they spent Sunday at the Library while Maureen stayed with Bean, who was up and around, feeling much better. The little Man was sore and had a bad headache but his spirits were high and he was especially happy to see his Aunt Mau.

It was the next Wednesday before Monica and Josh had a chance to think again about their next Service visit, this time to find Running Shoes for Monica. They were a few days behind their planned schedule but they had made allowances for the unforeseen. After classes they headed to Summit Sporting Goods.

Both Monica and Josh were really looking forward to getting back into the groove with their Project. Monica was excited about the thought of brand new running shoes and morning jaunts with sweet Koko. The time was right to rejuvenate and feel that rush again.

Josh had been an avid athlete before Bean came along. He still worked out at the gym every chance he got. Both he and Monica knew the importance of a good athletic shoe. It just made whatever you were doing easier and most important, the right pair of shoes enhanced performance.

"You're quiet JJ."

"I was just thinking about what you said that afternoon when I brought Bean home ... that he really is a special person, not just a kid, and that his being so amazing can mean great things for Bean one day. He has that contagious personality, a kind of charisma that you just can't get enough of. What you said that day really had an impact on me, in a good way."

"Oh, here we are!" beamed Monica. "Wish Bean was my little boy."

"So does he," replied Josh. "So, let's go and get you some decent runners." The twosome held hands, swinging them back and forth like two fourth graders as they found their way to Summit Sporting Goods.

"So far we've been lucky, not having to shop around all over the place for one thing, unless you count the Makeup Visit. But it was my choice not to shop somewhere else for makeup. I'd much rather have runners," Monica remarked cheerfully."

"Ya, well don't jinx it…let's hope they have the perfect runners for you…and here we are, the shoe floor…wow, lots of choice. Are you ready to get the best running shoes ever known to the human foot?"

"More ready than you know!" laughed Monica. A few days ago, Monica had purchased a running magazine, which contained advice about running shoes. Now, she just wanted to look carefully at all the styles, the brand names, the colours, and take it all in.

"I was thinking," she said, "that after this we could go and buy Beany some really cool T-shirts. I noticed that a few of his are pretty worn out."

"Bean has a dozen T-shirts and he only wears the ones you're talking about when he's playing or lying around the house. There's only one thing Bean wants and that's a…"Josh was cut off as a Sales Person approached.

"Hi there, can I help you folks or just browsing?" I'm Maxine but around here, they call me Max", she smiled.

"I'd love some help, Max. What I'm looking for is a pair of really good runners that won't give me blisters or make my big toe hurt ... actually both my big toes…the right one more than the left," pointed out Monica.

"Okay, I'd be happy to help you with that. If your big toes are hurting you, then it's likely because your feet are turning inward when you run," explained Max.

Monica was relieved and impressed. "Yes, according to my running magazine, that's what it said in there too. They called it 'over pronating', if your feet turn inward and it said exactly what you just said Max." Monica felt as if she was in good hands.

Maxine thought for a few seconds and then asked Monica, "Have you ever had any foot or ankle injuries or operations from an accident or something like that?"

"Yup," answered Monica. "It was a doozie too. I had a car accident and my ankle and foot had multiple fractures. There were a few operations and crutches…the whole nine yards."

Max was obviously concerned and thinking if there were any further questions she needed to ask before choosing some shoes for Monica. "So obviously that is what caused your over pronation. It's interesting that the toe that hurts you most is on the opposite foot, likely because it's the foot doing more of the work. OKAY then! I have some great shoes in mind for you. I'd also like to give you a shoe with extra cushioning and you will need extra stability to compensate for the over pronation of course." Monica liked the sound of that.

Maxine proceeded to measure Monica's foot and then left to get some running shoes. "I'll be back in a few moments. Can I get either of you a coffee while you're waiting?" asked Max.

Both Monica and Josh declined the offer, although both were impressed that they would be offered a beverage in a sporting goods store.

"Boy, she really likes her job and solving foot problems" remarked Josh. "She's good, really good. She's a veritable search engine of information on this stuff."

"She seems to really care too", remarked Monica. "I like her and I feel as if she likes me too. I think that's important."

"What's important Sweety?"

"That the Customer feel liked," repeated Monica. "It just feels good."

While waiting for Maxine to return, Josh was thinking about the makeup and makeover consultation. "Hey, what about that makeup you wanted?"

"Actually, I've been shopping online for makeup. I don't have time to go running all over the place for things. So I found a few places online and have been ordering a little at a time. They have these online questionnaires so you can see what colours best suit your skin tone and all that. It's kind of fun too."

"Boy, Zane's really screwed up that one," Josh whispered discreetly. "By the way, I've been meaning to ask you, did you ever find the Owner of Zane's, to meet with her or him?"

"Sure did. Sorry, I meant to tell you but we've been so busy with Bean and..."

"It's fine. What happened?"

"The Owner's name is George Ellis. I explained to him what happened and he seemed genuinely concerned. I was there for about 20 minutes. He thanked me for going to the trouble of contacting him and said he would look into the situation. He was a good Guy. I'm glad I took your advice about speaking to the Owner."

"So, would you return to Zane's?"

"I don't know. Maybe, maybe not. I just don't know yet."

Josh then printed the following in the Journal:

***"THERE AREN'T MANY SECOND CHANCES WHEN IT COMES TO SERVICE. IF YOU WANT TO KEEP CUSTOMERS, YOU'D BETTER GET IT RIGHT THE FIRST TIME! ONE UNHAPPY CUSTOMER CAN MEAN THE LOSS OF DOZENS OF FUTURE PURCHASES BY THAT INDIVIDUAL."***

Maxine returned with a mound of shoeboxes. Monica was really excited but she held back so she could focus on choosing the right pair. She grabbed her athletic socks from her bag, ready to try on the first pair.

As Max laid down the shoeboxes, she asked Monica if the socks she was wearing would be her running socks. Monica replied with a yes and told Maxine that she had three pair.

"Those are perfect socks for you," said Maxine, "because they have a cushion and see this stretchy part in the middle part of the sock, that will also help with the stability factor. Now your foot is a size 6 but I brought 61/2 because good socks like those take up a little space and we don't want your toes to be cramped. Plus the feet tend to swell while running. All the shoes I brought for you to look at have a rounded toe-box," Max pointed out as she removed the first pair from its box.

Monica tried on all five pair. She walked around the store in each of them and narrowed down her decision to two.

"I really like both of these. Do they come in any other colours?"

"They sure do," replied Max, as if she completely understood the importance of loving the colour.

"The only thing I want to point out to you is this," said Max, as she showed Monica the price tag on each of the two shoeboxes.

One pair was $120.00 and the other $150.00. "I just thought you should know the price in case you had a certain range in mind" she whispered. "Would you like me to see what colours I have in those two pair in your size or would you prefer to look at some others?"

"No, I really like both of these. If you could show me what other colours you have, in my size of course.

As Maxine headed back to look for some different colours for Monica, she noticed a woman looking somewhat annoyed. "Is someone helping you Ma'am?" asked Max.

"No....I wish they would though...I've been waiting here for ten minutes!"

Max ran to the backroom lounge, where two of the sales people were on break. She let them know about the Customer who was waiting, then quickly moved on to look for different coloured shoes for Monica.

Max returned with the different coloured shoes. She glanced over in the direction where the woman had been waiting and saw that Maddi was looking after her.

Maxine proceeded to show Monica both pair of shoes in different colors. "How do you like these colours?"

"Ooh, I love the pink/green combination and these are cute too, kind of a sunny yellow with purple accents." Monica was obviously thrilled with the choices. "Could I take a little run in each pair down the block? I'll leave you Josh and my purse as collateral," joked Monica, as she headed towards the door, waiting for Maxine's permission.

"Actually, that's a great idea. Sure, take them for a test run. You go Girl!" called out Max. It was apparent to Josh that Max was thoroughly enjoying Monica's excitement. First Monica took the pink and green runners for a test run; then she ran back and put on the yellow/purple pair. Off she went again, concentrating on every aspect of the shoes as she ran down the stairs, then down the block and back up the stairs, slightly out of breath.

"I really like the feel of this pair Max. I like the colour of the others better, the pink/green, but these are so comfortable. It's as if I'm on air! The other runners feel a little restricting."

"Makes sense," remarked Max, "That's because the pink ones have a higher stability factor whereas the ones that you said are more comfortable do have above-average stability but the focus is more on the increased cushioning. They are both really good shoes. I have another pair I could show you but they are over the $200 range and unless you're running marathons, they're probably overkill for your needs."

Monica had made up her mind. "Even though I like the colour of the pink and green ones, the yellow and purple is growing on me. They just feel more comfortable and cushiony. I'll take these."

"Josh budded in, "You're not just saying that because they're cheaper, are you?"

"No JJ, I really love the yellow/purple ones; the ride is awesome. They're perfect."

Maxine asked Monica if there was anything else she needed. She answered that she had all the other things she needed.... great socks, headbands, water bottle, tops, shorts, leg warmers and pants.

"Hey Max, whose the Manager of this Section" asked Monica

"Myself and Maddi. It takes two!" she smiled with a cute wink.

"So you and Maddi look after both the men's' and ladies runners," inquired Josh.

"Yes, that's right."

"Max, thank you, for taking such good care of me. It was really fun too."

"It has been my pleasure. I love Customers like you. Anytime I can help you out, let me know. Here's my business card. Thank YOU very much and enjoy your new shoes. They really look awesome on you and I think you're going to be very happy with them. By the way, I put a matching headband in your bag. We just happened to have one with the same colours as your new shoes, so I couldn't resist."

Monica was so happy about the whole experience that she gave Max a hug. "Thanks again Max," she shouted, as they left the Store.

"I'm actually loving these colours JJ. Wow, these shoes feel so amazing! I just love them!" Monica was obsessed with her new shoes and talked about them incessantly for the next five minutes, which led Josh to start thinking about running.

# Chapter 23

## One-Stop Mall

***"Mass advertising can help build brands, but authenticity is what makes them last. If people believe they share values with a company, they will stay loyal to the brand."***

***Howard Schultz—CEO Starbucks***

"Hey Monns, I think the running thing is a great idea. Thought I might join the club. I've decided I'm going to get some new running shoes too." "Josh, that's awesome! I think it would be great for you to do something like running. You should do something for yourself."

"The only thing is, I won't be able to run with you, because in the mornings I can't leave Bean alone. So I'm going to do my runs between 5 and 6pm if you could stay with Bean during those times."

"No problem, count me in!" Monica liked the idea of Josh taking some time for himself. "Anyway, it would give me a chance to have some alone time with Bean. How come you didn't mention it when we were in the Store?"

"Because I thought it would be good to check out another place for the Service Project. Then we'd have two different places to assess."

Monica was up for a visit to another store. "Smart thinking. Where would you like to go?"

" I thought we could go to One-Stop and see if there are any athletic stores there."

Monica was happy to do anything. She kept shifting her feet into various fashionable positions to see how they looked, while Josh drove to One-Stop Mall. They walked around browsing and searching for anything that resembled an athletic store.

"When you were doing your test runs, I phoned Mau and she picked up Bean. They're going to Bean's favourite pizza place for supper."

"Oh look Josh-----The EXERCISE BIN! Wow, that's a famous chain. I didn't know we had one here."

"Looks good," agreed Josh.

As soon as the Couple walked in, a good-looking, well-groomed Man came over and asked, "What can I do for you folks today?"

"Running Shoes...I need runners ... I plan to run about 3 miles a day and..."

The Salesman interrupted Josh, "Great, all of our men's runners are over here, if you would like to follow me. Here we are. Take a look and if you see anything you like, just let me know. I'll be close by. I'm Ivan by the way."

"Maybe you can help me out. I wouldn't know where to start with choosing a pair," said Josh, hoping for immediate assistance from Ivan.

"Sure, well, you were saying about three miles a day.... um, like do you want a firm shoe or well-cushioned shoes? We have all types."

"I'm not sure," answered Josh." Most of my life I've played sports and worked out but I haven't really done any serious running before."

"Well this style is very popular Sir and so are these," pointed out Ivan.

"I take a size nine I think," stated Josh. "I guess I'll try those two pair."

"OK, let me see if I have those in your size. You said a size nine, right?"

"Yup."

Josh and Monica sat down. "Not quite as sharp as Max so far, is he?"

"No...Cripes, that heavy metal music is giving me a giant-sized headache," complained Monica. "You'd think they could play some decent music."

Ivan returned. " I have one of them in your size Sir."

Josh tried on the shoes and walked about.

"They're a little tight and I'll be wearing thicker socks so maybe a half-size larger would be a good idea, plus we were told that feet tend to swell when you're running."

"Sorry Sir, those don't come in half-sizes. Shall we try a full size up? We have them in a ten I think. And you know, they will probably stretch. By the way, if you check out Drake over there—he's one of our sales representatives—you'll see that he's wearing this very pair."

Josh took a breath. Drake was black and the only black salesman he could see in the store. Feeling frustrated and tired, Josh decided to call it a day. "I think I'll give it some thought. In the meantime I should probably do some homework on the kind of runners I need. But thanks for your help and your time...Ivan."

"No problem Sir. Was there anything else you needed?"

"No thanks." Josh and Monica quickly walked out.

"Josh, why was he pointing to the Guy in the orange shirt?"

"He was just trying to be nice. Some people overcompensate; they don't want to appear prejudiced, so they come on too strong trying to be nice. I'm used to it. Let's go home. There's something I want to show you." Monica could sense the disappointment in Josh's voice.

Realizing Monica's concern, Josh reassured her. "Don't worry, I'll go to Summit and get some nice running shoes from Max tomorrow. But listen, right now I want to show you something important at home. I'm fine. I think you're going to love this."

# Chapter 24

## Two Tables

***"Quality questions create a quality life. Successful people ask better questions, and as a result, they get better answers."***

***Anthony "Tony" Robbins***

Bean was still out for dinner with Mau when Josh and Monica arrived home. Josh dropped his stuff and went to the kitchen to make some tea. Monica got settled and joined Josh where he was sitting at the dining room table already pouring their tea. There were some leftover muffins, which Monica brought to the table as she thought about how to begin the conversation. "I don't blame you for being upset with that guy at the Exercise Bin. He was downright irritating. But I know Max will find you a really great pair of shoes. Hey, you could shop online for your new runners, you know. There are tons of them online."

"You're right about there being 'tons'," replied Josh. "About three months ago I was looking for a pair of every day shoes. I went online. Must have looked at over 300 pair and I couldn't figure out which ones to get....too many. When I finally narrowed the field to a few pair that I did like, neither were available in my size. I ended up with burning eyes and a sore back. Online is good if you know exactly what you want, when you're looking for a certain brand and type...for me anyway. Anyway, I want to show you something important. While Ivan was talking, it hit me what the real difference was between him and Maxine."

Monica was intrigued. "Sounds like you've had a kind of revelation."

"More like an epiphany! Actually, this very table where we eat dinner, this table made me understand something. First, let's go look at the end table in the living room—your end table," snickered Josh.

"Hey, What's wrong with my end table? I like my end table."

Josh brushed his hand over his Grandmother's table, as he began to explain. "I'm dead serious here Monns. I think I'm onto something. See, our dining room table and your end table, they tell the story of the difference between Maxine and Ivan and even about the operation of the Stores where they worked. It's as clear as day to me."

"Josh....I'm not in the mood for guessing games. Explain please."

"OK, here it is." Josh removed the place mats and runner from the dining room table. He stood up, then put both his hands on his Grandmother's Table. It was as if he was preparing to give a sermon.

"MONICA, LOOK AT THE CHERRY WOOD ON THIS TABLE...LOOK CLOSELY. NOW, IF I KNOCK ON THE TABLE LIKE THIS...HEAR THAT? THAT IS QUALITY. IT'S ALL WOOD, THE VERY FINEST, THROUGH AND THROUGH IT IS THE REAL THING. NOW LET'S GO TO YOUR END TABLE...KNOCK, KNOCK....AHH, IT SOUNDS HOLLOW—BECAUSE IT IS HOLLOW!"

"OK, so one table is all wood and the other table isn't ... obviously," retorted Monica. "One is old, one is newer. Sorry but so what?"

***"Monica, it just isn't that simple. There's way more to it than that. The Cherry wood Table is AUTHENTIC, GENUINE. The End Table looks good...I'll give you that...but it's superficial; it won't last and it definitely will not be passed down through the generations like my Grandmother's Table. Somebody really went out of their way to make that cherry wood table. Look at the craftsmanship. Look at the care this piece was***

***built with. This cherry wood table...look at the detail work. It's PRICELESS! It's AUTHENTIC. It REEKS OF QUALITY!"***

***Josh continued, "The end table looks good on the outside but it's a phony...it's made to look like teak and tiles but it's neither. Whoever made this wasn't a craftsperson. They were a factory worker helping to put together thousands of other tables that look exactly the same as this one. Whoever designed your table designed it to look good, last a few years, as long as you don't put anything too heavy on it. Your end table is supposed to look real but there's nothing real about it. The company that made your table wasn't trying to create something special."***

Monica was now very impressed with Josh's observation. "I get it! What a remarkable comparison. ***YOU'RE COMPARING MAXINE'S SERVICE TO IVAN'S, AREN'T YOU?"***

"Yes ma'am! Maxine was really into it. She really did care, as did Ashleigh at Kat's. They delivered AUTHENTIC SERVICE." Monica was writing madly in their Journal as Josh continued. "Max went out of her way to get you the right running shoes. Her energy was awesome; she had this contagious enthusiasm in the way she talked and moved and she knew her stuff. Ivan was slick and polite but either he didn't know anything about running shoes or else he couldn't be bothered to do the work to get me what I needed. To me, that's PHONY SERVICE. That's why, for a purchase like running shoes, something that I'll use over and over again, I want Authentic Service. I want someone who really knows their stuff and cares that I get the right product--someone who goes out of their way to be a specialist. And I want somebody who has enthusiasm, the contagious kind. That is where Service meets Hospitality!"

"Think about the work Maxine did and how she let you go for a test run, how she cared about what kind of shoes you needed. You should have seen how happy she was for you when you were going for your test run. She was, without a doubt, truly excited and enjoying herself. MAX, LIKE MY GRANDMOTHER'S

CHERRY WOOD TABLE, IS ONE OF A KIND. IVAN, WELL THERE ARE THOUSANDS OF IVAN'S AROUND TO SERVE PEOPLE IN A MEDIOCRE WAY. But he did look good, I'll give him that much, like your end table."

"Okay! Enough about my end table. But you're right. You definitely have hit on something Josh. It's an amazing analogy."

Monica added, "Ya, Ivan was pretty cute and Max, no beauty queen. Appearances can be so misleading! You're pretty cute Josh—are you the real deal?"

"Very funny Monns, but not so funny if you spend money and end up with the wrong product, thinking that you've gotten a deal, only having to buy the same thing all over again, because you didn't get the right item in the first place."

" Two Tables....who would have thought so much could come from looking at two tables," reflected Monica.

Together Josh and Monica wrote it all down.

***TWO TABLES ANALOGY***

- ***Authentic vs. Phony***
- ***Effort vs. Laziness***
- ***Knowledgeable vs Ill-Informed***
- ***Caring & Helpful vs Cute & Slick***
- ***Sincerity vs Baloney***

***CONCLUSION: Authentic Service Will Bring Back The Customer!***

Monica was pumped. "This whole exercise was really important, notwithstanding your beating on my table. Josh, are you listening?" Josh had fallen asleep on the sofa. Monica threw a blanket over him. Then she wrote him this short note.

*"Hey Josh....I really love your two tables analogy.*

*I'm kind of excited about Service now. I'm actually glad we took this course! I honestly never thought I would be saying that!*

*Have fun getting your runners tomorrow..... Hugs...Monns"*

The next day Josh did go to see Maxine. Max was there and she gave Josh the same level of attention and service that Monica had enjoyed the previous day. Before he left, Josh went over to Max. "Hey Max, I just want you to know that Monica loves her new runners. We're doing a paper on Service and you got five stars from both of us. You're really good at what you do! You make your Customers feel...important.

Maxine was blown away and almost speechless. She thanked Josh. It was obvious that she was not used to receiving such positive feedback from Customers. She blushed slightly and told Josh he had made her day.

There was an extra spring in his step as Josh made his way to the parking lot. However, on the way home, he sensed something was wrong with "Red", his car. Josh brushed it off for the time being, figuring it was a loose fan belt or something. He relaxed and sang along to his favorite CD. It had been a great few days and a little rattle wasn't going to spoil it for him.

# Chapter 25

## Red Needs Help

The next day Monica arrived home looking very upset. Josh was busy looking under Red's hood. There was nothing owned by Josh that meant more to him than his cool red car.

"What's up?" asked Josh while peering under Red's hood.

"I'm just so pissed off." Josh closed the hood, realizing Monica was really rattled.

"Why, what happened?"

"I had an appointment to have my teeth cleaned with Lily and she kept me waiting 45 minutes. I asked the receptionist there how much longer she thought it would be after waiting twenty minutes. Oh, just a few minutes she told me. It was more like another thirty minutes. I sat there all that time, looking at out-dated magazines, thinking of all the stuff I had to do. Then finally I had my teeth cleaned and ended up missing part of a class. I mean what is wrong with these People! Don't they realize that patients are busy too! It's like they don't even appreciate that you give them your business! She's a hygienist; it's not like she has emergencies to deal with and after a decade of doing the same thing, she knows how long each appointment takes. I have to shake this off. It's just so maddening!"

"Sounds frustrating." As soon as he said those words, Josh knew it was a lame response.

Monica continued to blow off steam. "It's like you're sitting there and no one even acknowledges or cares. Then you become totally stressed because you know you should be somewhere else, plus it makes you feel like two cents. You feel invisible, you know. It's like you're nobody to these so-called professionals."

Josh recalled an incident where he had been kept waiting. "Yup, I do know that feeling...it's frustrating, you feel guilty because you're either missing something or have things to get done. You feel unimportant. Oh my poor Monns...come to papa for a hug."

"Thanks but I don't feel like hugging; I feel like biting somebody. When things like that happen, receptionists should be honest. They should apologize and give you a chance to make another appointment. At least they should tell you the truth about how long it will be and give the person waiting some options."

"Yes my little vampire, but If they did that, they could get a lot of flak from their bosses. I say it's the bosses who should tell them how to handle a situation like that, the way you just described--be honest and if the person wants to reschedule, well at least you still have a returning patient. If that receptionist had any guts, she would have told you the truth and explained later to the hygienist."

"It just makes you want to scream, especially when you have a lot of things to get done. You're sitting there, thinking of all the things you should be doing and the people working are just so used to seeing people waiting, it's as if you're a piece of the furniture to them. It will be some time before I ever go back to see Lily again, if I ever do go back. All she talked about, while my mouth was open, was how busy she was and her new car." Monica stopped. She could see that Josh looked worried about something and he had some grease on his face and hands. "What happened? Here I've been babbling on and..."

"It's Red. I took him to the dealer where I usually go for an oil change. They told me the problem was probably with the transmission. Now they want to take the car apart and do a diagnostic. So I just checked under the hood and found a loose fan belt. I just don't trust those guys. You would think that when they changed the oil, they would have at least seen the fan belt! Or maybe they did see it and then forgot about it. Just feels to me like they're looking to make some money with the transmission talk. Red is six years old but that's not so old for a car these days. I need someone I can trust to recommend a place to have the car checked out. They charged me $350 bucks for an oil change, new filter and to top up some fluids. Like, who can you trust with your car these days?! With cars it's like you fix one thing and then that reveals other things and more things; it never ends. It just pisses me off that these guys get away with charging prices like that and giving all kinds of BS. I'm definitely not going back there again!"

"JJ, we need to find someone you can trust to check out Red before the 'on and on' scenario begins. Guess we both got two phony 'tables' today."

Of course Josh knew that Monica was referring to the substandard service that both she and he had experienced that day. He was pleased and somewhat surprised that she remembered his analogy, especially after such an upsetting day.

"Good one Moni and true. Some people just don't know or care how customers think. What good does it do them to be like that? Fools! They just end up losing customers!"

Monica grabbed the Journal and wrote that down.

"Monns, you just gave me an idea! We could make our final Service visit to a car mechanic we can trust. The only problem is where am I going to find someone like that?" Josh paused, as if he was remembering something. "When I was trying on running shoes with Max, I tried on this blue and red pair and that reminded me of Red. So I started talking about Red to Max, telling her I was a little concerned that something wasn't quite right with him. It was really cool because as it turned out, she's really into cars. She talked circles around me...talked about cars I've never heard of. Anyway, Max mentioned a place where she always brings her car. Some mechanic named...Ma...Mar--it's on the tip of my tongue--Matthew! His name is Matthew! She really raved about this guy."

"Where does he work?" asked Monica, still writing in the Journal.

"I don't know but I sure am going to find out."

Monica had something on her mind that she had wanted to ask Josh for a while.

"Josh, I need to ask you a personal question."

"Sure, what is it?"

"Remember you used to call me MJ and sometimes you even called me by my second name."

"Uh huh, I remember."

"Why did you stop calling me MJ or Janine?"

"Another time Monica, please...not now. I have to check on Bean."

The next day Josh went to see Max around lunchtime but she wasn't there; it was her day off. Josh asked the salesperson at the register if she had ever heard Max talk about Matthew."

"For sure, Matthew looks after my car too. He's a genius!"

"Where's he work?" Josh asked. "You're Maddi, right?"

"Yes, hi. Matthew owns his own place. It's not big but he's the best and really honest too. You can find his place at the end of The Pike where it turns into the Highway." Maddi then drew a map. "It's about a forty minute drive and it's called 'Matthew's

Garage'. His place is kind of set in, so you have to watch for it. Here's my card. If you have any trouble finding it, just give me a call. I'm here until 6pm. And by the way, all of us bring our cars to Matthew and so do my Folks and my Brother and everyone in Maxine's Family. You'll see. Matthew has a magic touch with cars and with people too."

"I really appreciate it Maddi. Thanks very much." Josh felt reassured and hopeful. On the other hand, he wondered if it was too good to be true.

# Chapter 26

## *The Matthew Event*

After their next class, Josh and Monica left to drive Red to Matthew's Garage.

"What do you picture Matthew looking like Josh?"

"Um, let's see. He's Italian or Spanish or maybe Mexican, has about fifty years of car experience, a really wrinkled, weathered face, a slight limp and he's about thirty pounds overweight, slow-moving, waddles a bit because of a war injury, but methodical and knows his stuff. How's that?"

Monica laughed. "A slow-moving, wrinkled, overweight, waddling, albeit knowledgeable mechanic...I don't think so Einstein, except for the 'knowledgeable' part. You're a hoot, you know that?"

As Josh was driving, he thought it was time to answer Monica's question from the night before. "Moni, the reason I stopped calling you MJ or Janine was because I was really ticked off when you were living with those other guys...both of them. They didn't treat you right. I was angry with you for not seeing that. Calling you MJ or Janine just reminds me of those two jerks because, well you know why."

"Yes, I know, because Roger liked the name Janine and Marty called me MJ."

Josh paused and thought for a moment. "Look Monica, it doesn't matter. What does matter is that you're my best friend and hopefully I'm your best friend. We're there for each other. We give to each other what the other needs when times are tough. That's what friendship is. I'm not angry about it anymore, just glad you came to your senses."

"I think you've given to me more than I've given to you", declared Monica. Like the way you had my back at Rascal's and you're sharing your home with me and...wait, turn right! There, over there... see it?

"I see it--Matthew's Garage. Made it! Good boy Red. This car always comes through for me. Thanks, I almost missed the turn."

As Josh pulled into the driveway, coming towards them was a middle-aged man who definitely did not look like Josh had described. Matthew was tanned, with weathered skin, about Josh's height, with a friendly, middle-aged face and in good physical shape—no waddle and no apparent war injury.

The driveway entrance was bordered on each side by tall green, chain-linked fencing with Poplar trees peering over the fence from one end to the other. Just past that, there was an open field, about three acres, with cars parked neatly as if they were on display, about fifteen of them, mostly from the twentieth century. Some of the cars were fifty or more years old. It was quite a site for any car lover, which Josh certainly was. The garage was A-framed, with a green roof and white aluminum siding. There was a grassed area to the right of the mechanic's garage, with a green picnic-style table. Further over to the right was a lovely, quaint A-frame log home, decorated with wildflowers all along the front.

Josh got out of the car and approached Matthew who was wiping his hands with an oilcloth in the driveway.

"Hi," said Josh. "You were recommended to me by a few of the People at the Sporting Goods Store. I'm Josh and my friend

Monica and I were wondering if you could help us out with some car problems." Josh waved to Monica to come over, which she did. I probably should have called first."

"Ah, Summit Sporting Goods" replied Matthew. "I never go anywhere else for that kind of thing. Good people those Summit folks. Don't worry about not calling. You caught me at a good time."

Monica came over and joined Josh. It was a beautiful sunny autumn day.

I'm Matthew Mazzetti."

"Mazzetti? Are you Italian?" asked Monica hopefully.

"Yes Miss, on my Father's side; my Mother is from France…why do you ask?"

"My Mother is Italian. So I guess we're of the same vintage, sort of," Monica commented shyly.

"It is a pleasure Miss Monica. When I saw your beautiful red car pull up, I just had to come out of my garage….beautiful paint job. You cannot beat Ferrari Red." Matthew gave the car a big Italian style kiss, expressed with a hand to mouth smooching sound, as if he were tasting a fine wine. "Bella Tesoro!" he declared.

Josh looked at Monica for a translation.

"It means treasure," replied Monica, who always took pride in being able to translate.

"That is right," chuckled Matthew, obviously impressed by Monica's understanding.

"Thanks very much!" Josh was very proud of his car. He had put a lot of work into its appearance over the years--a wood veneer dashboard, a wooden steering wheel and newly upholstered tan and black checked seats etched in black leather.

He had chosen a special paint and paid dearly for it to be done properly.

"Tell me your problem Joshua," Matthew said already on the ground, peering under the car.

"All I know Sir is I have a loose fan belt but something else is wrong. Someone at another place told me that the problem was with the transmission. They changed the oil, topped up all the fluids and charged me a pretty penny too. I was told by Maxine and Maddi that you're very knowledgeable and honest. So here we are."

Matthew asked Josh to drive the car into the garage. When Josh got in there, he thought he was in tool heaven. "Wow, look at all these--man, how long have you been doing this?"

Matthew responded proudly, "With my own business, almost fifteen years with other places, ten years, so about twenty-five years in all. When it's my birthday, my family knows to get me tools. There is nothing better than a fine tool. For me it is as important as a surgeon's tools. Cars need the right tools…this I know."

Josh was already beginning to have great admiration for Matthew but he was concerned about the cost. They only had about one-hundred dollars left in their project fund. Yes, he knew he had extra money in the bank, thanks to his Grandmother, but Josh had very specific plans for that money. As he was mulling this over, Matthew offered them some tea. Both Josh and Monica declined his kind offer but not before Monica mouthed silently to Josh "Whoa, Tea?" Their facial expressions exposed Josh and Monica's surprise at being offered tea by a mechanic.

"Listen," said Matthew with obvious sincerity, "I would love to help you but the only thing is, I do all my own work and as you can see I am already working on several other cars. If you can give me three or four days, I'll be able to help you and will let you know what is wrong with your car and how much it will cost to fix it. If you like, I can loan you one of the older cars there while you leave your car here. As long as it is here, I may be able to look at it sooner. One never knows because I may work on a car that I thought would take one hour and end up spending seven hours on it. You understand what I'm saying?"

Josh was somewhat sceptical and unsure if all this charm was real or just part of some sort of con. "I do understand. That is very kind of you." Josh felt he had little choice at this point.

"You are welcome. Let's just go over some things here, just to make sure I understand fully. I always like to go over everything with my Customers. Come, come to this bench over here…my office I call it. First I'm going to make some tea for all of us. Do you like tea?" asked Matthew, looking at Monica then Josh. Both nodded graciously. "I'll bring milk and sweetener and you can make it the way you like it." Matthew left to make the tea.

"I love his Italian accent," commented Monica.

"Do you buy all this Monns? I mean who ever heard of a mechanic serving tea. Oh, and he loves my car. Of course he loves my car. It needs work!"

"Josh!" Josh wasn't listening. "JOSHUA, listen! I really think this guy is for real."

"Monica, you would think Lucifer was the Savior if he put on the right costume, , had an Italian accent and offered you some tea."

"Okay, okay…so I'm more trusting than you are, maybe even a little naïve. But I really think this Guy is the real thing. Give him a chance. What choice do you have anyway? Both Italian and French men are, for the most part, very charming. It's the way they were brought up to behave. Look at all the cars here and remember what Max and Maddi said. Everybody isn't a con artist Josh. All these cars are here for a reason."

"I know that. Look, when I go to a restaurant I expect great service. But when you go to a place that fixes cars, oh sure, they're nice enough but this is a little strange."

"Strange just means different. And in this case, I like the difference. Everyone thought Van Gogh was strange. You're stereotyping. I really hate when you do that. You of all people should know better. How about "All Black men are…"

"Oh man," interrupted Josh. "You crack me up sometimes. Sorry, I'm not going to ask how you would have finished that sentence. Point made. I surrender. I'll just go with it and we'll see what happens. As you said, what choice do I have? And no more stereotyping. What would I do without you to keep me decent?"

"Exactly right," boasted Monica cheerfully.

Matthew soon returned with a tray, a large teapot, sugar, honey, milk and some homemade sugar cookies—'his Mama's recipe', he boasted.

The three sat down at the picnic table. Matthew pulled out a binder and pen. "Tell me what you have noticed about your car that concerns you. Describe the problems to me."

Monica pulled out the Journal. This was amazing she thought--Matthew wanting to LISTEN to Josh, the Customer. Imagine that! she wrote. She tried to contain her enthusiasm. In her mind Monica wondered, how did this man learn to treat customers this way? Did it just come to him naturally or had he found a formula for providing outstanding service? Of all people, she didn't expect this from a Mechanic. There's that stereotyping, she reflected, wanting to kick herself for even thinking that a Mechanic wasn't capable of providing great service. This guy was just so focused on helping Josh out. Monica could not get over his understanding of people.

It occurred to her that this experience with Matthew was beginning to epitomize the name of their Course, that this is what the Professor was thinking when he called it, 'HOSPITALITY & SERVICE—WINNING OVER THE CUSTOMER'. She quickly added in their Journal, "We're being won over by Matthew's authentic and hospitable approach."

Josh had let go of his scepticism and was now obviously enjoying every minute of the attention he and his car were receiving from Matthew. He began to describe to Matthew the problems he had been noticing and experiencing with Red. His doubts about Matthew were quickly falling away.

Josh began, "OK, well first and foremost, the car's steering is a little loose and it vibrates. And then there's the loose fan belt of course, which is probably the cause of that annoying squeaky sound. Then I have noticed that the headlights sometimes dim and the gauges on the dash board kind of flicker. The people at the other shop topped up the steering fluid but the problem is still there with the steering."

"That's good, a very good description," remarked Matthew while taking some notes. "So, there are three things you have noticed about your car which concern you. There is the loose fan belt, the loose steering and then the dimming of headlights and flickering gauges. Is that correct?"

"Yes," replied Josh "That's it, to the best of my knowledge."

Monica was writing madly, "Matthew repeated what he heard Josh say to ensure correct UNDERSTANDING of the problem."

"Wow!" eked out of Monica's lips mistakenly. Both men looked at her wondering what she had seen.

"Oh, sorry....It's this tea Matthew. It's just so delicious but very hot!" commented Monica, trying not to laugh out loud at herself.

"More tea?" asked Matthew as he filled up Monica's cup before she had time to answer.

"Thank you Matthew. Josh, that's so great that Matthew can loan you a car while Red is being fixed up."

"So Josh," continued Matthew, "I know you're a student and students usually do not have a lot of money. I sense your concern about the cost and I don't want you to worry. You're a nice couple and I want to help you out the best I can. Would you like me to go ahead and check out your car?"

"Yes, that would be great. What do you think the problems are...do you think they're serious?" The cost factor was indeed bothering Josh.

Matthew looked at Josh's tires as he began to answer. "The steering problem sounds like you have a wheel alignment issue...that's not so bad unless you leave it too long. The good news is that your tires are in good shape, lots of tread; they're good tires. So, if it is the alignment, that is not so expensive. As for the flickering and dimming issue, I think that is your alternator. I know that sounds big but it's not as bad as some other problems, believe me. But if you leave it too long, that also can make big problems for you. The fan belt is easy to replace. Your description was very helpful Joshua. But first I check out the whole car and then I call you with an estimate after I know what is wrong."

"That sounds good Matthew."

"Joshua, your car is beautiful; as I said, it is a Tesoro. I can tell when someone loves their car and cares for it. Of course, that is why you are here. At least, I hope that is the reason."

"Yes, that and the fact that I have a Son. I mean I don't want to drive a dangerous vehicle with my Son in it, you know. So I need to make sure that it's fixed properly."

Monica enjoyed listening to Joshua and Matthew talk. She could tell that Josh was feeling a lot happier.

Matthew put his hand on Josh's shoulder. "You and I, we both are working very hard. It was very good of you to tell me about Max and Madeleine's nice reference too. Every time I get a new Customer, it feels like a gift to me. That is really how it makes me feel. I love the work I do and most of the people I meet. It's in my blood, this car business. I want you to be happy when your car is all fixed. I will call you once I look over these problems and I will check out the whole car. So maybe if I do a good job on your car, you will recommend me to someone else. In the meantime I have met a very nice couple so it makes me extra happy that you brought your Red to me. One thing you will know when I call you is this, I won't give you any phony baloney."

"I like your philosophy Matthew. It's been a real education here today with you. I feel as if my car is in the right hands," acknowledged Josh.

"Gracie Joshua, so give me your phone number so I can call to give you the analysis of what I find and an estimate." I very much appreciate that you trust me with your Tesoro. So maybe when you come back, I can meet your Son?"

"Of course," replied Josh. "Bean would love to see your Place."

There were handshakes all around and then Matthew pulled Josh aside and whispered, "Your Girlfriend, she's a keeper. I'll be in touch and don't worry Joshua."

"Miss Monica, it was a pleasure to meet you. You are a beautiful and charming couple and I am going to do my best for you. That you can count on."

Once they got in the car, Monica started writing like a fiend. She noted some further points which she sensed were key to their analysis of this special visit.

"What are you writing?" asked Josh.

"Everything that just went on…Wow, like if that wasn't AUTHENTIC SERVICE, then what is!" declared Monica.

"True," agreed Josh "But what's it going to cost? Let's wait to assess this one until we know the cost factor. I'm beginning to think you were right. We may have lucked out and found a rare and caring soul."

# Chapter 27

## *The Diagnosis*

A few days later Matthew did call Josh as promised. Josh braced himself. He knew it would likely cost more than $500.00 but that was about all he could afford or else he would have to change his plans or sell his music system.

"Hello Joshua. This is Matthew calling."

"Oh, Hi Matthew."

"Joshua, it is as I thought. I have checked out your car and the problems you are having are with your wheel alignment and your alternator. We should replace your alternator and fix the alignment ."

"What about the fan belt? asked Josh

"Forget about the fan belt; I already replaced it for you."

"Oh, thanks Matthew. Um, how much do you think it will cost to align the wheels and install a new alternator?

"It will cost you about $650.00 plus tax. The breakdown is approximately$400.00 for the alternator installed and $250.00 to correct the alignment, give or take a few dollars--the estimate is within five per cent. How does that sound to you? I throw in the fan belt, no charge. If you need to pay me over time, monthly payments for three or four months, that is fine. Do not worry about that."

"Thank you Matthew. Can I get back to you in about ten to fifteen minutes? I'm just in the middle of something here with Bean. I'll call you shortly."

"Fine, of course," replied Matthew.

Josh immediately went to the internet to check out the average price for wheel alignment and alternator installation. He found that Matthew was about $50.00 above the average price of both. He then thought of the $350.00 he had spent at the first place that had serviced his car. They did nothing in comparison, plus they never even called with a quote. Josh also considered the fact that Matthew had checked out Red thoroughly plus it seemed he had accurately diagnosed the problems right away. Another place would likely have charged for hours of diagnostics. Josh concluded that Matthew's quote was fair and likely less than he would end up paying somewhere else. He wanted the job done right rather than looking for a deal from someone he couldn't trust. Yup, everything pointed to Matthew being a man of principle and integrity, not to mention that he was obviously a brilliant and gifted mechanic.

Josh then called back Matthew and asked him to go ahead and fix Red. Matthew was very pleased and told Josh that Red would be ready by 9am Saturday morning.

When Monica arrived home, Josh explained to her about Matthew's call and the cost. She had actually prepared herself that it would cost more. She insisted on putting in $50.00 and although Josh protested, Monica's insistence was unstoppable. With $50.00 left in their Project fund, even with tax added, this would leave Josh only $75.00 to $100.00 short of what he had put aside for car maintenance. They would just have to do without their weekly pizza nights a few times that month. That would take care of it. Josh breathed a sigh of relief.

"When do you want to meet to discuss our visit to Matthew's place," asked Josh.

Monica looked at the schedule. "Let's see, our schedule says we should meet with the Professor early next week, to find out about the Assignment. We're pretty much on track, which is terrific, don't you think? But we should make allowances for the unexpected."

"Uhhuh…my Italian task-master," kidded Josh, tossing throw cushions at Monica and Bean.

"Oh Beany, what are we going to do with your crazy Dad?"

On Saturday, Bean joined Josh and Monica when they drove to pick up Red. Josh was right. Bean ran around looking at every car at Matthew's place. Matthew loved watching Bean. "When I was a little boy," remarked Matthew, "I was like that. What a wonderful Son you have Joshua. You should be a proud and happy Papa to have such a smart and good-looking Son."

"I am." replied Josh, "I'm proud and gratified. He really is a special kid."

Josh and Matthew completed their transaction and chatted for a few moments. In fact the total cost was about $20.00 less than what Matthew had quoted. Josh thought it best to pay the full amount now.

"Joshua, thank-you for trusting me with your car. I want you to be happy with my work. So if you have any problems, you call me or come straight in and I will make it right. But I say this humbly…I think you will find that your car now drives like a dream because I took the liberty of taking it for a little test drive. I think you will be pleased. It is important that you are happy with the work."

"Thank you so much Matthew." The two men shook hands and Matthew waved goodbye to Monica and Bean. Matthew watched them leave until they turned onto the main road. Josh had an unexpected feeling, as if he were leaving a friend.

"You were right Monns, about Matthew. I'll be bringing Red, and any car I have when Red's time is up, to that Man. But he is strange..."

"Joshua stop that."

"Strange as in extraordinary," grinned Josh.

It was definitely time for a drive along the Parkway. As they drove Josh listened carefully...no squealing, no vibrating or loose steering, and no flickering on the dashboard gauges. Boy, thought Josh, the steering has never been better. It was smooth driving at every turn.

"Wow! Red has never run better you Guys. "YAHOO! I HAVE MY CAR BACK!" Josh was on cloud nine. "What a beautiful morning!"

The Threesome headed home where they had sandwiches for lunch. Monica had been writing at warp speed in their Journal. She and Josh planned to meet shortly after lunch.

# Chapter 28

## *A Leap of Understanding*

Monica opened the conversation with a look of intensity as she raised her hand, pointing her index finger upward, just as her Mother always did when she had something important to say. "Josh, this Man, Matthew, this Man has lived his adult life for the love of cars and people. He is in a whole other league from anyone who has served us. MATTHEW IS NOT A REPLICA OF YOUR GRAM MAYA'S TABLE. HE IS YOUR GRANDMAMA'S TABLE, AS AUTHENTIC AND JUST AS EXTRAORDINARY. He is one in a million, like one of the finest bottles of Italian vintage wine, Elio Altare's Barolo Brunate—I forget the year—but oh my, those who really know their vintage wines would give this wine a score of 95, a very high score for wine. Matthew deserves no less in our assessment of him. I do not consider myself a connoisseur of Service but from what I do know and have learned about it with you, Matthew is at the top of his profession, because of his unique and genuine way with Service and because of his deep love, passion and knowledge for what he does, authentic well beyond words. It all comes from his heart and his soul in a profession that is not known for these attributes. I could see these qualities with every word and every move he made. He is a Tesoro, rare and precious."

Josh was speechless. How could he match the poetic language, the passion and the knowledge that Monica had just shared with him?

"Monica...that was beautiful and moving." He gazed at his Friend with fresh eyes. She had such passion and wisdom, which he had failed to notice before. How could he have missed those special qualities, he wondered. Josh realized that he had not been listening hard enough, that he had not given Monica the time she deserved to express herself. Josh always knew she was perceptive and caring but he had never heard her speak with such passion and authority. Perhaps, he thought, this was just the right time or maybe she just felt such a special enthusiasm for their encounter with Matthew that it stimulated this unforeseen eloquence.

"I know you took a lot of notes when we were with Matthew," remarked Josh. Is this a good time to share more of your insights with me. You're really on a roll, that is, if you're not too tired. I can't believe it's only noon.

"Now is the perfect time." Monica smiled. She was both cognizant and uplifted by Josh's understanding of the depth of her expression. "I have something else in mind for this analysis," she added.

"Great! I'll get us some tea." Josh was excited. He felt completely energized. It was no longer just a college project. It was like a plate full of your favourite foods, waiting to be tasted.

# Chapter 29

## *High Noon*

Monica was thinking of a way to encourage Josh to talk in depth about their experience with Matthew. She wanted him to open up, especially in this case, since she sensed that there had been an unspoken connection between Matthew and Josh. With Josh feeling so upbeat, she thought this was a good time for him to open up about the experience.

"So, what I thought would be really helpful is if you told me how you felt and what you were thinking during our visit to Matthew's. I'll ask you questions, you answer them as fully as you can, and I'll take notes while you're talking. How's that sound?"

"That's an easy one Monns. In a word I thought that Matthew's Service was GREAT! Listen, I forgot to get some books for my Accounting assignment, so I thought that after our tea, I'd just scoot over to the Library. We could meet after that."

"But you were the one who was excited about doing this now. Can't you get the books later? The Library's open until 11pm."

"Monica, we're talking an hour, ninety minutes tops. Relax, it's no big deal."

"Oh boy, here's the old Josh. I wondered how long it would

take for him to show up. Go, go, if you think it's more important than this."

"That's not how it is. I love this Course and this Assignment and you know it. This Service Assignment is important but it's not my life. I just want to go to the Library. I'm not going to Switzerland! Why are you being like this? You're not my Mother." Josh regretted that last part as soon as the words fell out of his mouth.

"Lord help the woman who is! What happened to you between making tea and sitting down here? You were all revved up. You said you loved what I said about Matthew. It's like you're two different people! Whatever Josh, w h a t e v e r!"

"What happened was that you started telling me, again, how we were going to do this part of the Assignment. You talk to me sometimes like I'm a little kid. 'Oh Josh, I'll ask the questions and then you'll do this'. That's crap! Did you ever think I might want to be the initiator, for once?"

"Fine. Excuse me for trying to keep us on track and excuse me for caring about this Assignment and excuse me for asking to hear what you had to say. I thought this really meant something special to you. Go! I'll stay with Bean. Just go."

"I do appreciate how hard you've worked on this Monns and it does mean a lot to me but you have to let me breathe. That doesn't make me a bad person."

"No, it just makes you an unreliable one...go, go and breathe!" Josh left.

# Chapter 30

## *One Giant Step*

Once Josh was out the door, Monica went to her room and let the tears flow. She punched her pillow several times and cried into it, hoping that Bean wouldn't hear her. She got up to check on him and saw that he had fallen asleep. Exhausted from the argument, she lay down beside him and drifted off.

Josh emerged at about 2pm, where he found Monica and Bean sleeping, only this time it was Monica snuggling Bean's stuffed turtle. Josh was holding yellow roses and a tub of Rocky Road ice-cream.

"Hey, you two," he said softly.

Bean woke up first. "Hi Dad. Where were you?"

"I was at the Library." Monica opened her eyes, looked at Josh, saw the roses and ice cream and turned the other way.

"MJ, I'm sorry for being a jerk." Reluctantly, Monica turned towards Josh.

"Did you two have a fight or something?" Bean asked, rubbing his eyes.

"Yes, kind of," admitted Josh. "I got some cones too so we can make ice-cream cones. Bean, could I have a minute with Monica."

"Sure Dad. I have to go to the bathroom anyways."

"I got you these yellow roses, your favourite."

"I see that. Thank you," Monica made brief eye contact with Josh.

"I'll be in the kitchen. Please come. I have something important to say to you."

Monica went to her room to brush her hair and then refreshed herself before making her way, reluctantly, to the kitchen.

"I know you like to eat ice-cream out of the tub. Here you go, dig in." Monica had misgivings and declined the peace offering, just as Bean was entering the kitchen.

"I have something private to say to Monica." began Josh nervously. "Here's your cone Beanie."

"Can I watch one of the Hobbit movies Daddy? I know how to put it in."

"Sure. Call me if you need help with the settings."

"I know how to do it. Aunt Mau showed me and to tell you the truth, I'm not crazy about these kinds of serious talks."

"You're not crazy about them?" You got that expression from your Aunt Mau, didn't you?" Josh chased Bean, picked him up and roughed him up like a puppy, all the way to the movie shelf. Monica waited, not thinking about anything in particular. She felt numb and apathetic. Josh returned to the kitchen. He sensed what was ahead.

"Sorry Monns, I am truly sorry. Please, just listen to what I need to say to you."

"I think you said it already. You were perfectly clear."

"No, I was an idiot. I was the old Josh, doing what I wanted and not caring about my commitment to our meeting, which I had led you to believe was very important to me. I let you down because I felt like going for a drive in Red and the Library was the perfect reason."

"Oh, so it wasn't really important to you...it was just an obligation."

"Hear me out. I'm not as articulate as you are, especially when I'm nervous. After I went to the Library, I drove around and I realized that in a way I was avoiding some of the most important points about this Course. See, until now, I saw service as something we watched others do for customers."

"Get to the point Josh. What does this have to do with what you said to me?"

"You inspire me Monica. You really do. And that's scary sometimes. What I realized was that if you're going to bring serving others into your life, that should start with the people who mean the most to you. You have to show those people through your everyday actions and words that they matter more than anything or anyone else. Service is about making people feel good about themselves. You do that for me and it scares me sometimes. You reached out to me and I rewarded you with stupid, inconsiderate words. I am so sorry. I can't tell you it won't happen again but I can tell you, that if it does, I'll make it up to you because you deserve to be treated like a princess. So, just let me know when you want to meet about our Matthew visit and I'll be there, as long as I don't have a class."

"Josh, I just need to go for a walk to think things over. I appreciate what you just said. I'll see you soon. I'm still a little groggy from my nap."

Monica returned about a half-hour later. Josh was watching the movie with Bean. She joined them for the rest of the movie.

"Monica, are you and Dad still having a fight?"

"No Beany, we're fine. That was a good movie, huh? Monica

looked at Josh and smiled. "How about tonight?"

"Okay." Josh was relieved.

It was just after 8:30pm when Monica joined Josh at the Table. She could smell the scent of coffee brewing.

"Where do you want to start?" she asked. Josh could see that Monica was still bruised from their argument.

"Well, I'd like to start the way we usually do. I like the process."

"You're so weird. Okeydokey. I'll get the coffee." As she did that, Monica noticed that Josh had placed the roses in a vase, in the middle of the Dining Room table. She broke a smile and Josh smiled back, as they each poured their own coffee.

"I know you can be very articulate JJ. After all, you're the one who came up with the Two Tables analogy. That was brilliant. I'd like to know what you thought and how you felt throughout the experience with Matthew and I need you to put those thoughts into sentences, not single words like 'great' or 'amazing', like the way you did with the two tables analogy."

"I'll try. It's not always easy for me to understand my feelings, let alone describe them. Let's see, a good description of how Matthew made me feel." Josh clasped his hands and began to focus. "Alright, let me try to explain. See, Gram Maya was a really special person. When I look at her Table, I remember all the things I loved about her. She made me feel as if I was really special to her. She listened to every little thing I said or asked. She always answered and not with clichés either, like the other adults in my life did. It actually made my Mom a little jealous I think. Anyway, let's not go there. So, that's what the Table means to me. That's what Matthew did, see. He made me feel... important, as if my headaches with Red really mattered. My headache became his and he was determined to fix Red, and confidant too. It was real. He loved my car, despite my cynicism about that at the time. I could tell he really did think

Red was a masterpiece. He asked me questions and he really relaxed me, because he LISTENED to what I had to say. Not only did he listen but it was obvious he UNDERSTOOD how important this was to me. Also, THE WAY HE TREATED US, like we were at a Bed & Breakfast! He really blew me away, even if I didn't show it at the time. I mean we didn't even call first--talk about hospitality! Now I get it, Hospitality…How To Win Over The Customer. I mean we just showed up, he dropped what he was doing and spent an hour with us. Who does that these days? Overall, Matthew made me feel important and welcome, and he convinced me that he legitimately cared. I only wish that Judith at Zane's had been willing to drop what she was doing for you. There, how was that?"

"Heartfelt, specific and captivating," responded Monica gently. "How did you know Matthew cared JJ?" I felt that too but what did he do to make you so sure that he cared?"

"I knew he cared because he asked the right questions, then he took notes…just his whole demeanour. It was just so obvious that Matthew was totally committed to helping us. He made a diagnosis after he listened and he turned out to be right with that diagnosis. He knew his stuff too…that's really important! He was real, like Gram Maya and her Table…he's a priceless original. Oh, and all those tools, I could see that they were really well looked after. He had a special place for each of them. That showed me that he was meticulous and took great pride in his work."

"To me," continued Josh, "It was like a CONSULTATION SESSION but with no forms, all personalized and tailored just for me and Red. That's how it felt.

I actually enjoyed myself. I mean how often does that happen—having fun bringing your car to a mechanic?"

"Wow!" Monica was truly surprised. "You explained all that so beautifully. Now that was real. I really get why Matthew won you over."

"Okay, let's continue. How about the cost? Did you think that was fair or too high or what?"

"Well I'd say we got FULL VALUE AND THEN SOME. Maybe it was a little more than others would have charged but not enough to make me go somewhere else...I'd go back to him and only him for any car problem. I TRUST HIM. You know it has been a long time since I FELT REALLY APPRECIATED during a transaction. Knowing that your business is really appreciated feels great. The whole experience was really special. My initial cynicism turned out to be completely wrong. So how did you feel about the experience at Matthew's?"

"I had fun there. I felt a lot of the same things you just described. Maybe I didn't feel as important as you did but what I did feel was INCLUDED. Sometimes when two guys are discussing things like cars, they just look at each other when they're talking. But I HAD A SENSE OF WELL-BEING, because Matthew made sure he connected with both of us. You know, the Italian connection. I felt as if he liked both of us. For me, IT'S IMPORTANT TO FEEL LIKED when I'm a customer.

"Right," acknowledged Josh, "It's like when you got your running shoes, Max made me feel included. That's an important point."

"JJ, it's time to go and see the Professor. We need to find out about the Report thing . Professor Sydney is a pretty crafty Guy. I bet he has something deliciously fiendish in store! I want ours to be the best."

"It's going to be the best Monica, because together we're unbeatable!"

"Welcome back JJ."

# Chapter 31

## The Great Assignment

***"You have to learn the rules of the game. And then you have to play better than anyone else."***

***Albert Einstein***

The day had arrived when our Twosome would meet with Professor Sydney. Josh gathered up all the receipts as Monica picked up their Journal and the two nervously proceeded to his office where they found him reading. After a quiet knock on the door, the Professor got up and invited them in. Josh and Monica reintroduced themselves as he showed them into his office. He then offered them coffee. Monica and Josh both accepted and thanked him. Nerves made them both thirsty. The Professor asked his Teaching Assistant to bring in the coffee, which he did. Josh then gave the Professor the receipts with a brief explanation regarding Matthew's Garage, explaining that only $50.00 from the Project money was used towards that particular Service experience. The Professor was fine with it.

"So then," asked the Professor, "You have completed five experiences?"

"Actually Sir," replied Josh, "We completed seven; one of them was unplanned and just sort of happened with my car insurance. "

"Oh my, then I owe you $50.00," stated the Professor.

"Not really, Sir," responded Monica. "We didn't spend any

money on the car insurance experience, except for a stamp," she laughed nervously.

"Well then, I owe you $25.00 for certain. Here you are," smiled the Professor. Josh and Monica thanked him and then in unison, took a sip of their coffee.

"Professor Sydney, have there been many of the twosomes here before us, from the Hospitality Course?" asked Monica.

"You are only the second couple to have come in so far and I can't say I was very impressed with the first," he responded with unexpected candour.

"In any case, Ms. Flowers and Mr. Johnson, let me ask you an important question. My question is, why, from a practical standpoint, is it essential to win over the customer? Why don't you answer first Mr. Johnson."

Josh thought for a few seconds. He wanted to express this intelligently. "First of all Sir, if the Customer is not won over, he or she will likely not return to that establishment. There are few second chances to impress."

"Ms. Flowers, can you add to that answer?"

"Yes, Sir. If the Customer is not won over, they will not speak well of the establishment, which means that the establishment will neither build nor maintain a good reputation. That inevitably inhibits sales growth."

Josh thought that Monica's answer was far better than his. For some reason, that didn't bother him. He accepted the fact that Monica had a gift for expressing herself with a particular eloquence.

"Well," chuckled the Professor, "We are off to a dandy start, aren't we? Yes exactly right, both right. Simple isn't it…then again, not so simple in reality. As the CEO of a very successful Canadian hardware company said, 'It's a battleground out there'. His company started in 1964 with one Store and now it's a 20 billion dollar a year success story, built on delivering personal customer service. You have to be smart and care to the hilt to be successful in business today. This CEO went undercover to some of his company's stores, worked side by side with the employees. He returned with a far greater understanding of what his people needed in order to provide the kind of customer service he was aiming for. For example, how could employees provide great service if they could not easily find products in their warehouses? So he brought in inventory devices for employees. That solved the problem. He saw where the problems were in service and discovered some great employees, whom he subsequently rewarded. It's a smart thing for CEO's to do, especially in large companies. This CEO knew, even from his desk, that Customer Service was the prime ingredient for success. Unfortunately, for many Owners and Directors, service excellence remains a secret ingredient, yet to be discovered."

Monica and Josh hung onto every word. "Professor Sydney," uttered Josh, "It has been a real eye-opening experience. If I ever own a business, Customer Service would definitely be my first priority."

"Yes, service excellence is a special experience isn't it. Very glad to hear that Mr. Johnson. In any case, about your Assignment, which I will explain to you now--I also have a handout for you. You will write your Report together and you will present it together as well to the entire class. So, there are two parts to this-- the writing and the presenting. I think you will find this to be a very worthwhile experience."

Both Monica and Josh were glued to the Professor, as if every word would determine their future success.

"For the first part of your Assignment, the written part, I am asking that you write about each experience and that you do so in such a way that it becomes an informative and interesting Presentation to the entire class. Be as precise and insightful as you can. Together you will present your insights in a manner that will enable your fellow Students to absorb the information to the highest possible degree. How you do this is up to you. The Presentation cannot be boring or elementary. It should be meaningful and noteworthy. The goal is that your Presentation will teach and leave a lasting impression on the other Students. In the process, as you organize and synthesize your experiences, you hopefully will recognize certain aspects, which thus far have eluded you."

You could hear a pin drop at this point until Josh and Monica both shifted in their chairs simultaneously.

"Is that a Journal you have there Ms. Flowers?"

"Yes, Professor, it is our joint Journal, describing details and insights about each of our Service Escapades," replied Monica proudly.

"Escapades ... excellent term," chuckled the Professor. "And a very good idea to keep a Journal of your experiences. I sense that you have made a good team. Well, that is certainly a key to success in life. Very good then, do you have anything you would like to ask me at this time?" The Professor then gave Josh and Monica the written instructions for the Assignment.

Josh did have a question. "Sir, regarding our Presentation date, will it be posted?"

"Yes, I will be posting those dates on my door before the end of this week. If I were you, I would start working on your Assignment as soon as possible.

After a few more factual questions, Josh and Monica left and continued their day with their normal class schedule. They agreed to talk further that night about the Assignment.

Before they parted, Josh could tell Monica was feeling nervous. "Don't worry Sweety. We got through the first part of this. The second part will be a breeze in comparison. We can enjoy the process and do a great job."

Monica appreciated Josh's confidence and encouragement. To her, this Project had become intensely important. She smiled when she thought about how well she and Josh had done in the first phase of the Project. And now, more than ever, she wanted the second phase to be powerful and inspiring. Monica could think of little else the entire day.

# Chapter 32

## *Reflecting & Preparing*

The time had arrived for Josh and Monica to begin planning their Presentation. They had EXPERIENCED service and hospitality in several different forms. They had REFLECTED UPON and ANALYZED each experience. They were anxious to put it all together.

One day when they were deciding on the format for their Presentation, Monica told Josh that their work together had inspired her to "be less in my head". She wanted to look beyond herself, a quality she saw in Ashleigh, Maxine and Matthew. One of Monica's best qualities was her desire to do better, always. When she talked that way, Josh would say that she was being too hard on herself and although she enjoyed his confidence in her abilities, she couldn't help but judge herself repeatedly. The differences in each of their personalities caused them to plough through many their discussions, but they both knew that too was part of the learning experience. Sometimes they reached a consensus. Other times, Josh or Monica would make the stronger point, and the other would yield. It wasn't easy. However, the challenging process created some pretty bold and exciting insights.

By Thursday the dates and times of the Class Presentations were posted on the Professor's door. Monica and Josh already knew that they had been selected as one of the five couples doing their Presentation to the Class. Their Presentation was scheduled to be in about three weeks' time. It would be the final one.

Together Josh and Monica went over their Journal, adding notes as they read through each of their Service Escapades, talking, discussing and sometimes shouting. Finally, they were able to put together a draft of their Presentation. They each worked on different sections and then showed each section to the other. Once the draft was completed, they reviewed, edited, tweaked the tweaks and finessed it until they felt completely happy and comfortable with it. The tweaking seemed endless, until finally they recognized that their final product was ready for the next step, rehearsing. As they rehearsed out loud, they kept adding, deleting and tweaking, a word here, a phrase there and then, it was done.

In the meantime, the class Presentations had already begun. There were three Presentations that really impressed them. Jocelyn and Koko had put together a real razzle-dazzle production, using PowerPoint images and some strobe lighting. It was full of humour and some good stories.

"I thought that the bank visit described in their Presentation was just outstanding. Wish we had thought of going to a bank JJ."

"And, holy crap!" whispered Josh, "They mentioned which bank too! Guess that bank won't be seeing too many incoming Clients from Horizon once the word gets around. Man, Jocelyn and Koko were right on when they explained how today's student could be tomorrow's success story and how many of those success stories there have been. They really did their homework. And so did Barry and Meg. What I liked about their Presentation was the unique places they visited and how they pretended to be tourists when they visited the Tourism Centre."

Monica agreed. "I also liked the Presentation by Richard and Lainie. Their life experience made that one more special, the way they personalized the information really made me think.

It grabbed my attention. Those two really have vision. It was pretty great. I hope ours comes across as well as theirs did. The only thing that disappointed me was how a few people didn't take the Assignment seriously, namely Larry and Ross."

Josh was now focused on their own Presentation. "Hey Monns, what do you think of me asking Maureen to read over our Presentation? She'd be straight with us. "

"Great idea...I like the way Maureen thinks. You know Josh, she's really good to you."

"Ya, Mau's the best. I just wish she could find someone. She told me that her dating life is practically non-existent."

"Josh, have you thought of maybe buying Maureen a gift, to thank her for all of her help. Who wouldn't want a sister like that?"

"I should. I think sometimes I take Mau's help for granted. I am going to do that...definitely going to get her something nice and not just this once either."

Monica was deep in thought. "What are you thinking? I know that look...what's in that head of yours?" asked Josh reluctantly curious.

Monica did have that look, the one that meant that she was having an 'AHA' moment.

"I know what we can do with the $25.00 the Professor gave us!" Monica shared her idea with Josh.

"That's a brilliant idea! I' can do that. That will just make the Presentation! "Nice going. You're on fire, Girl!" Josh was pumped. They both were.

Maureen did read the Presentation and loved it. She also had some great suggestions.

By the time the morning of their Presentation arrived, Josh and

Monica both felt ready. They wanted their Presentation to be good enough to inspire their colleagues. They desperately wanted it to be the best one. It was obvious that they both had developed a passion for this subject. But would that passion come through? Would people see how their experiences had affected them? They were both focused, centred and determined as they headed to Horizon.

# Chapter 33

## *The Power of Service: The Presentation--Part 1*

The Professor introduced Monica and Josh to the Class as he had done with each Couple who had made a Presentation. Our Couple had set up their notes and materials prior to the class. They had requested two easels the day before. The Professor made sure two were there for them. On each easel Monica had placed two large posters with only the blank backside showing. They had their two podiums beside each other, only two feet apart, with one easel on either side of each podium. Behind them they had a striking banner, which they had made together, hanging from the whiteboard. The banner read:

### *THE POWER OF SERVICE*

***MONICA:***

Good Morning Professor Sydney and Fellow Students. To tell you the truth, when I first heard the Professor tell us about this Assignment and then read the instructions, I was far from excited. Josh, my Partner, was somewhat more optimistic. Never in my life have I been so wrong. This Assignment turned out to be one of the best learning experiences of my entire life. It is our hope today that we  can share our journey with you in such a way that you will understand why both Josh and I are so enthused and inspired by what we call, our 'Service Escapades'!

Storytelling is one of the oldest forms of communication. We have chosen storytelling as our mode for sharing our Escapade experiences with you. We hope you enjoy it.

**JOSH:**

Our Escapade was not easy and sometimes we were truly frustrated. However, about half-way through our journey we made a discovery that we would like to share with you. We call our discovery

'Two Tables'. The symbol of our Two Tables embraces and conveys the true power of service.

> *(Josh then turned around both posters on the easels. One was an enlarged photo of his Grandmother's Table; the other was a photo of Monica's End Table. This was the idea Monica had shared with Josh, to take photos of the two tables and enlarge them, using the $25.00 which the Professor had given them).*

This one is a picture of the Table left to me by my Grandmother, Maya. This table is Cherry wood through and through; it's an ORIGINAL. It's AUTHENTIC and totally GENUINE.

Now, let's look at the table pictured on the other easel. It's supposed to look like teak and tiles but it is neither. The table is as light as a feather. IT'S A PHONY. It was manufactured along with hundreds or more like it. IT'S SUPPOSED TO LOOK REAL BUT IT ISN'T REAL AT ALL.

To Monica and me, that is the difference between mediocre, average service and superior, fantastic service---the first is PHONY; the second is GENUINE.

**MONICA:**

Our journey taught us how special and fantastic service felt and looked. It also showed us what poor or average service felt and looked like in comparison.

Josh and I have used the image of these two tables because it reminds us of the difference between the two types of Service. Whoever built the cherry wood table was truly dedicated to excellence. That person obviously took pride in their work and cared tremendously about the quality of the finished product.

That, ladies and gentlemen, is what it takes to deliver extra-ordinary service BUT, it is just the beginning!

Josh and I both agree that service is more important than we ever could have imagined—it is a powerful force that does not receive the attention it deserves. "It's a battleground out there," as the CEO of a large, successful Canadian company said. You cannot even compete, let alone win the battle, if you do not build your business on the shoulders of Customer Service. For that reason and many others, the awareness and execution of Service and Hospitality must be raised to a far higher level than the status quo.

***JOSH:***

As we take you on our journey, we hope you will gain a further appreciation for the huge impact that Service has on all of us. Like Monica, before this Project, I had no idea how essential and valuable Service and Hospitality are to a thriving society or why.

Before we made our first visit, we decided what our Mission would be.

***Our Mission Was To Learn the following:***
***What Customers Think, What They Want and How to Give it to Them. We also discovered along the way the Why. Now, you can judge just how successful we have been in accomplishing that Mission.***

Let's begin with our first visit, which was to Kat's Seafood Paradise. The thing about Kat's that really caught our attention was that everything, absolutely everything, was geared towards the Customer having a pleasurable experience, from the decors, which included a stunningly beautiful aquarium, to the way Managers backed up their Servers and Servers backed up each other. They did everything and anything to make sure no Customer was left unattended and, they were so upbeat in the process. We saw at Kat's that great Service is a mentality. Monica and I experienced that wonderful, infectious mentality, which is why we had such a great time there.

It was as if the whole Staff at Kat's was into 'Service beyond Borders'! Regardless of how busy any Staff Member was, they seemed to thrive on it. They were all about Service and Hospitality, making us and everyone else there feel happy and at home. That contributed to the atmosphere as much or more than the beautiful decors. It was as if 'Thinking Like a Customer' was intuitively in the veins of every individual who worked at Kat's. And you know, when we first arrived there, I was worried about my Son. I felt guilty about not spending enough time with him. But after a short while, those worries had disappeared, because of the fantastic service and hospitality we experienced there. That is the Power of Service!

The truth is, that when Monica first brought up the phrase, 'Thinking like a Customer', I made a few disparaging remarks about it. I was so wrong. IN FACT, THINKING LIKE A CUSTOMER IS THE SOUL OF GREAT SERVICE.

***MONICA:***
The second person who served us at Kat's was a Manager. Since Ashleigh was very busy, the Manager quickly picked up on that and offered to take our order. That was the first sign of Teamwork. Kat's could have used another Server or two that night. However, that did not diminish the quality of service we received, not one bit. There was such synergy, that just watching all the Staff and Managers support each other, made the service experience even better.

We were so impressed, that during our analysis session, Josh and I concluded that it is better to have fewer staff, people who really love to serve customers, who do it well and who care enough to back up each other, than to have more staff who don't care and don't deliver that exceptional experience.

There was an obvious pride among the Employees at Kat's. They had a kind of rhythm going, as if it were all choreographed. In short, it was awesome!

When the Manager came to take our order, we weren't ready and that is when he said something that I will always remember .He said, "WE'RE ON YOUR TIME MS. FLOWERS, NOT OURS." Can you imagine how that made us feel! From that point forward, we were totally relaxed. If that's not made to order hospitality, I don't know what is! Neither Josh nor I had ever heard anything like that before.

Thinking like a Customer also means understanding the importance of the little things. Ashleigh gave Josh and I two mini-sized bottles of champagne to have with our coffee and dessert. She wrote us a thoughtful little note. Also, you know how when someone has served you, they say the same old thing like "Have a nice evening" or "Have a nice day"? Well Ashleigh closed off with something more original. She said, "It really has been a pleasure serving you. I hope you will come back to see us," and she gave us a big, SINCERE smile. It just did not come off as cliché. It felt real and genuine because it was. The little gestures and words, the way we were treated…these were the things that made our night, even more so than the delicious food.

Kat's restaurant and Ashleigh in particular did something very important...they made us feel as if we really mattered! Customers Want To Feel That They Really Matter.

And here's the other thing we discovered at Kat's: we expected it to be great but the whole service & hospitality experience went far beyond our expectations.

That is one of the most important discoveries we made throughout our journey, THAT BETTER THAN EXPECTED SERVICE BRINGS CUSTOMERS BACK.

And of course, that is the whole point--to inspire customers, not only to return but to do so more often.

WE SAY, THOSE ESTABLISHMENTS WHICH DO DEDICATE THEMSELVES TO DELIVERING SERVICE BEYOND EXPECTATIONS, DESERVE TO HAVE THE MOST CUSTOMERS.

The two things that have lingered on well past this wonderful visit are: the incredible Teamwork we witnessed and those remarkable words, 'We're On Your Time, Not Ours'. Those are words you might expect someone to say to a celebrity or to a loyal, affluent customer. Those words made us feel special. THAT OF COURSE IS THE KEY—TO MAKE SOMEONE WHO FEELS ORDINARY FEEL IMPORTANT. That is what genuine service and hospitality are supposed to do.

***JOSH:***

Our Second Experience was very different and poles apart from our experience at Kat's Seafood Paradise, which really was like an evening in Paradise. Although our next escapade didn't bring us to the depths of perdition, in no way, NO way, did it live up to even our most modest expectations.

> *(As Josh was speaking, Monica looked around the room. All eyes were focused on Josh. She glanced at the Professor and even his eyes were peeled on Josh. The Professor looked rather pleased she thought...hopefully.)*

***MONICA:***

Our second visit was to a local drugstore. I was obsessed at the time with buying new makeup and having a makeup consultation.

In retrospect, there was a kind of omen as we began to enter the drug store, in the form of a sign that directed us to use another door. I just found that so annoying and inconvenient. It later brought us to a discussion about the importance of easy access for Customers. Access should be targeted to the needs of Customers, not to whatever is convenient for the establishment.

It was all uphill after that.

When we approached the makeup counter, two Staff Members continued chatting while we stood there for what felt like an eternity. When you're standing and waiting, five minutes feels like fifteen! Okay then, I thought, 'Get over it Monica....you're here to have fun buying some makeup and to get that consultation you've always wanted'. That did NOT turn out to be the case. Being kept waiting is so infuriating, especially when there is no good reason for it and no apology.

Now, had I gone into this drug store knowing exactly what kind and colour of makeup I wanted, there would have been no problem. But that was not the case. I wanted recommendations on what type of makeup and which colours I should be wearing. As it turned out, the Beauty Consultant admitted to me that she didn't know much about their makeup products because, she said, no one had trained her. Apparently she had been there about three months. Furthermore, she obviously had not taken the initiative to learn anything about their makeup. She was clueless! So, first she kept me waiting while she was chatting it up with another employee, then after waiting, she informed me, albeit politely, that she didn't have the knowledge to help me out.

I felt sorry for her that she had not been trained but at the same time, I was angry that she didn't have the moxie to even have tried to learn on her own. Not knowing what to do, she paged her Supervisor. Then I thought, 'Yay, someone who knows their stuff!' Yes, well that part was true. However, as it turned out, the Supervisor was far from accommodating. You see, I had interrupted her administrative work. Did I mention that this visit was on a Friday during mid-morning, when one would expect customers, not admin work to be the priority? The Supervisor tried to book me for that afternoon at 1pm, but I had a class. She would not budge. No doubt, she was on 'her time', not mine. The Supervisor's demeanour was officious and icy. By then I had enough. In fact, I was so disappointed and upset that I asserted to Josh, 'A Spit on Them!' It is an expression that my Mother uses when she is seriously upset. That Supervisor just would not put down her clipboard to accommodate me.

The words "We're on your time, not ours", spoken by the Manager at Kat's, those thoughtful words rang in my head over and over after that experience. What a stark contrast between Kat's Seafood Paradise and that Drug Store!

Since we left there, I have not returned and will NOT go there for anything more than a package of mints. However, it was a perfect example of Horrible Service and Zero Hospitality. As for shopping for makeup, I now shop online for beauty products.

Regardless of how badly a service experience may go, it is critical to customer relations that when we serve others, we always cross that finish line with grace. We must leave the Customer feeling uplifted.

IT'S NEVER TOO LATE TO TRY AND DO EVERYTHING YOU CAN TO TURN THINGS AROUND, FROM BAD TO GOOD. IT TAKES A CARING, SENSIBLE AND COURAGEOUS PERSON TO DO THEIR UTMOST TO FIX A MISTAKE. WHAT BENEFITS ARE THERE TO NOT CARING ENOUGH? NONE WHATSOEVER, NOT FOR ANYONE.

Subsequently, Josh made me realize that if I really cared about the quality of Service and Hospitality in New Plateau, then I should do something about it. After we discussed some options, I decided that making an appointment with the Owner of that Drug Store would be the best idea. That's what I would want an unhappy customer to do if I were the owner. I did that and you know, what really surprised me was that when I came face to face with the Owner, and explained my experience at his Store to him, he was gracious, listened and thanked me for going to the trouble of coming to see him. As yet, I don't know if anything has changed at that Store but I do know that I tried to help the situation improve for future customers. I still doubt I will give that Store a second chance. That is why it is so critical to deliver super service and heartfelt hospitality. Had it not been for that very disappointing experience, I likely would have returned to that Store several times by now.

***JOSH:***

If you had observed Monica after her drugstore experience, you would have seen how a bad service experience can destroy a Customer's whole day. It exhausted her.

While Monica was waiting to be served, I took a tour around that Drugstore. What I saw was some very apathetic employees who were not at all interested in the needs or well-being of the customers; they didn't engage customers; they didn't look at customers. Can you imagine treating guests in your home that way!

Furthermore, it is a very sad thing when a Supervisor puts down a customer rather than putting down her clipboard. Someone at the top needs to retrain their management people or develop new managers who want to put customer service first. The whole scene was an embarrassment, not only to that establishment but also to New Plateau!

We learned how impressive service can make a person feel buoyant and cheerful—that is NOBLE POWER. But, a disappointing service experience that can cause a person to feel lethargic and heavy-hearted. That, Ladies and Gentleman, is CRUEL POWER.

# Chapter 34

## The Power of Service
## The Presentation--Part 2

***MONICA:***
Now for the incident that caused Josh to have a conniption.

***JOSH:***
I wouldn't go that far.

***MONICA:***
Really? The Dictionary says that a conniption is a 'fit of rage'. What would you call it?

***JOSH:***
I would call it, 'a reasonable reaction to a ridiculous run-around'. You see, it began when I wondered if my car insurance rate would be lower, since I had recently turned thirty. So I phoned my insurance company to find out. Their voice mail system is simply ridiculous. After being asked three sets of questions and having to click a selection for each question, I was then transferred by the Receptionist to an Agent who said he did not cover my region. Following that, the Agent transferred me to the right person, but it turned out that person was on vacation. And here's the part I love the most--the voicemail message of the person who was on vacation, referred me to the Man who had just told me he did not look after my region. It was frustrating, time-consuming and insane.

I call it voicemail madness. This time wasting run-around made me so angry that I just couldn't take it anymore. If that's a conniption, then I plead guilty. People want to be served by people, not by automated messages. Automated messages were invented to be helpful, not to be a menace to busy, well-intentioned customers.

I almost ended up going down there myself, until Monica stepped in to help. She told me about a reputable insurance brokerage company, so I phoned them. The brokerage company was very helpful and I spoke with a real person. He made the whole thing easy for me. Shortly thereafter, I received a very nice, informative, upbeat letter from him explaining that I could save $180.00 on my car insurance, plus he recommended an insurance company. They did all the legwork and all I had to do was sign two pieces of paper. My insurance is now close to $200.00 less.

What a difference between the run-around I experienced at, what was my insurance company, and the efficient, helpful, personal service I received from the brokerage company. It was amateur versus professional service, or to put it another way, it was phoney versus genuine service, like our Two Tables. Company X's service was inconvenient, impersonal and slow. It may serve their needs but it certainly is not tailored to the needs of clients. And hospitality? Well, there just wasn't any at Company X, not on the phone anyway. But isn't the phone-in Client just as worthy of great hospitality and efficient service?

What should Company X have done? First of all, they should revamp their voicemail system. It's way too complicated. Secondly, I should have been transferred to someone who could have helped me. If he or she wasn't there, then someone should have asked what the most convenient way was to reach me. Or, the Man who said I was not in his region, could have looked up my information and called me back. Had someone shown an interest in helping me, I very likely would have stayed with Company X.

When people in a company pass the buck, that often means no bucks at all for them. Company X blew it. I could have been a client of theirs for fifty or more years.

***MONICA:***

After that experience, we wanted to do something different and it was! Josh set up an appointment to meet with one of the Directors in the Department of Tourism. I was present but this was primarily Josh's gig.

***JOSH:***

As Monica said, I set up this meeting to obtain information about Tourism in New Plateau and I was pretty excited about it. Actually it was after this experience that I began thinking about my Grandmother's table and how it represented something important but it took this visit and two more before I pieced together the overall relevance of the Two Tables.

Back to our meeting with a Director at the Department of Tourism. Several members of my Family work at our major tourist attractions which increased the importance of this meeting for me.

Those Family members who work in the Mountain-Climbing and downhill ski areas, have told me that tourism has not increased. That is one of the major reasons I wanted to know what plans are in the works to bring more visitors to New Plateau.

Here we were, going to a government department seeking information about the City we live in, the City where Monica, our Families and I have been tax-paying citizens for many years.

The Director came out of his office to greet us. That felt great. Once we were seated in his office, he gave us a file which contained pamphlets and some magazines, with ads for New Plateau's attractions, and a report on strategic planning. That did not feel good because, except for the strategic planning report, the rest was old hat.

When I asked the Director about new ideas or mentioned other projects I had read about for New Plateau, he went on the defensive, explaining all the problems and challenges involved with bringing in and accommodating new attractions. It was clear that the Director had no intention of listening to what I had to say nor did he seem to care about my interest in tourism. By this time in our meeting, Monica was working at smothering a yawn. It was morning and we would have loved some coffee or even water. But alas, none was offered.

Here's the issue that really frustrated me. The Director had little or no knowledge about their website ... he brushed it off! Can you believe that in this day and age! This was the Director of Communications for Tourism! Not only did he show little interest in their website, he used the excuse of not being computer savvy as his primary reason for not caring more about it. So he left that work to his IT Man. I wanted to yell, "Wake Up Man! It's 2014! People who are looking for places to travel to, generally look at websites first!" Of course, I didn't say that. I was speechless.

Now, in his favour I will say it was good of the Director to meet with us. In his own out dated way, he was trying to be helpful by having a folder of information put together for us and he was courteous, although not to the extent of being hospitable...no coffee or water offered and no real two-way communication.

Sometimes people in positions of authority become so accustomed to TELLING, they forget to LISTEN. Feeling heard lets guests know that their questions or opinions matter. And who knows, when we listen, we may not always agree but afterwards we often think, 'Hey, that person had a good point'.

So, you might be thinking that not everyone is a great communicator but do you not think that is a primary prerequisite for a Director of Communications? Furthermore, can you imagine a Director of Communications not having hands on knowledge of their website? How can you successfully promote tourism if your website is not one of the main tools you focus on to do that?

I took a Course once on the topic of 'Listening and Communication', and it really had an impact on me.

I LEARNED THAT WHEN YOU REALLY LISTEN, NOT ONLY SHOULD YOU BE FOCUSED ON THE PERSON SPEAKING WHICH THE DIRECTOR WAS, BUT ALSO,YOU SHOULD ACKNOWLEDGE WHAT YOU HEAR IN A WAY THAT WILL LET THE PERSON KNOW THAT YOU UNDERSTAND WHAT THEY HAVE SAID. YOU DO NOT HAVE TO AGREE BUT YOU DO NEED TO SHOW THAT YOU HAVE HEARD THEIR POINT OF VIEW. WHAT YOU DON'T DO IS GO ON THE DEFENSIVE.

Feeling that you have not been heard is frustrating, insensitive and definitely not hospitable.

It's easy to get bogged down in the reasons why something cannot be done. It becomes a state of mind. That is where many people stop, at the problem stage. But that is not how progress happens. Progress comes from getting passed the problems and coming up with answers, so that good ideas can be implemented. Moreover, you cannot open a locked door without a key. You can't surround yourself with the same people every day and just talk about the negative things, like lack of productivity or reasons why no one will go for a great idea. You have to find ways to reach beyond that. You don't get out of the swamp by seeking help from people who are in the swamp with you. You have to care enough and if you do, you just might inspire others to join you. Sound idealistic? Tell that to the Wright Brothers and Alexander Graham Bell or Martin Luther King or Oprah Winfrey. We need some movers and shakers to change the mindset of those who are in charge.

For me our meeting with the Director was a big disappointment. But who am I...simply a resident of New Plateau who happens to care about our economic strategy, in what is one of our foremost sources of employment and growth. The Tourism Director is a Civil SERVANT. Who are he and the politicians serving? So, do we just stay with the status quo where our Civil Servants and elected officials live, and continue to do the same old thing to protect their jobs? Or do we ask those people to implement ideas that will create growth and improvement?!

Professor Sydney stood, "Mr. Johnson, Miss Flowers, let's pause there for our break. Everyone, please be back in 10 minutes."

# Chapter 35

## The Power of Service
## The Presentation--Part 3

**MONICA:**

Our next two escapades were both related to shopping for running shoes. The first of these was an inspiring experience. It brought our understanding of service to a whole new level, because the service was completely different from anything I had experienced before.

I ended up with the perfect pair of runners but unfortunately Josh didn't, at least not on that day.

How many of you have purchased Athletic Shoes for some sort of athletic activity?

OK that's about twelve people. How many of those who raised their hands have received what you would call expert service to help you choose those athletic shoes?

One person--Russ, did you get your shoes at a sporting store?

"Actually Monica, I had to get them custom made at a special orthopaedic place because of a serious operation I had on one of my feet."

So did the rest of you who purchased running shoes buy them at a Sporting Goods Store?

I see nods from many of you.

Well, do I have news for you People! Josh and I went to Summit Sporting Goods where we were approached fairly quickly by a salesperson whose name was Maxine. I highly recommend her. Maxine's service not only won us over but we also learned a lot about service that day. I never imagined that a shoe salesperson could make a difference in my life. But that is exactly what Max did.

Never mind Max's great personality and helpfulness but also who knew that there was so many factors involved in choosing the right running shoes!

First, Max asked me what I needed the shoes for. Once I explained that to her, she asked me if I had any orthopaedic problems, to which I answered yes and I explained what those problems were. She then determined that my feet were over pronating, which for those who don't know--I certainly didn't--means that my feet turn inward when I run. Max explained that If I'm not wearing the correct type of running shoes, even for walking a mile or two, this causes certain painful problems. It is because of these problems that I stopped running in the first place. I wish someone like Max had been around to advise me years ago. I had read a guide on selecting the correct running shoes, in a running magazine. However, I found the article somewhat confusing and very technical, and there were too many choices of shoe brands named. Max was not only knowledgeable, she was also crystal clear in her explanation.

She then proceeded to measure my foot and was VERY precise. Max then left and returned about ten minutes later with several boxes of shoes. Here's the kicker about this one. Once I had narrowed down the search to two pair, I asked Max if I could take each pair for a one block test run. Max had no problem with that request at all. In fact, she applauded it.

By the way, Max also pointed out the price difference between the two pair I liked. Anyway, when I returned from my test runs,

I chose the pair I liked best but I didn't care for the colour. So Maxine searched at the back to see if that shoe was available in other colours in my size. It was. No laziness there. Max seemed so willing to run back and forth. I really felt as if I was in the finest of hands.

All this took close to one hour. I honestly felt as if I had been to a foot specialist. The care and concern that Max showed me were unprecedented, in my experience anyway. I just will not go to anyone else for running shoes or for anything else in the department which she manages. I have already recommended Max to several of my friends.

MAX MADE MY DAY! When we left, both Josh and I felt energized. I was absolutely ecstatic!

LET'S JUST SAY I NEVER IMAGINED THAT BUYING A PAIR OF RUNNING SHOES WOULD TURN OUT TO BE AN EXHILARATING EXPERIENCE THAT TRIGGERED GREAT MEMORIES!

***Josh:***
After we left Sporting Goods, I also wanted some new running shoes and I wanted to go to Max. However, it seemed like a good idea for the sake of this project, to try out another store, so we could compare the two service experiences. We may as well have been comparing a Ferrari to a scooter!

You see the Man who served me at this other sporting store, well, he was polite alright. In fact, he kept calling me 'sir'. He was also very quick to ask us what we were looking for, so his response time was very quick. And those are the only good things I have to say about his level of service. He was slick, you know. He had all the lines like "These are our most popular runners right here". However, Mr. Slick didn't ask me one question. After seeing what depth Maxine had gone into with Monica, the contrast was as stark as day and night. I think he may have been a quasi-racist too. But even if I am wrong about that, all I wanted to do was get out of that place.

That experience drove home the fact that being polite is not enough. Someone who serves you has to go out of their way. They have to ask you questions and listen to the answers. They need to actually care, not just pretend to care. Anyone can see through that. I chose to get out of there even before I tried on any shoes, but I did finally purchase some runners later that week, from Maxine. She gave me the same high level of service that she had given to Monica, although fortunately, I do not have any foot problems. Max must have brought me ten pair of running shoes to try on! It was a fantastic experience and fun too.

MAX HAS THIS WAY OF UNDERSTANDING PEOPLE. I BELIEVE THAT IN ORDER TO THINK LIKE A CUSTOMER, THAT INTUITIVE UNDERSTANDING IS THE ESSENTIAL INGREDIENT.

The other experience with the slick sales guy, that left me feeling so let down. It even affected my self-esteem. Fortunately, with Monica being so excited at the time about her new footwear, it was hard to remain solemn for very long.

Once we arrived home that day, I sat at my Grandmother's Table. That is when the TWO TABLES image hit me, the difference between Max and Mr. Slick.

You see, Monica's Table is hollow; you knock on it and it makes a hollow sound. It's a fake but looks nice, just like Mr. Slick. Monica's  table won't last. It's supposed to look real but it isn't real at all. There are many of these tables around just as there are many Mr. Slicks who go through the motions of serving people, but their heart just is not in it.

Now my Grandmother's Table, that's something you can treasure and be proud of. Somebody crafted that table with real pride and care. When you knock on it, you know that it's cherry wood through and through, like Max. She was the real deal, genuine, authentic - whatever words you want to use, she was absolutely committed and worked hard because it mattered to her that Monica ended up with the right shoes. She cared and didn't want Monica to reinjure her foot because of inappropriate footwear. She also cared that Monica had the best running experience possible. And when Maxine served me, that same care for her Customer came through in spades.

***Monica:***

THERE RARELY ARE SECOND CHANCES WHEN IT COMES TO SERVICE. Authentic service will bring back the customer. Mediocre or bad service hurts a business. It means that the business often has to compensate in other ways, like lowering the quality of their product, having sales or promotions they can't afford, paying employees less and therefore often settling for less qualified and less committed employees. That, my friends, shows us once again, the true power of service!

BOTH ASHLEIGH FROM KAT'S AND MAXINE FROM SPORTING GOODS TOOK A SYSTEM AND PERSONALIZED IT, EACH DELIVERING THEIR OWN SPECIAL BRAND OF EXCEPTIONAL SERVICE. The ambience at both of these Places was different for sure. But in both cases, the Managers and Staff were busy but enjoying their customers. We give the prize for Teamwork to Kat's because everyone there was totally involved in service and teamwork. Both places probably could have used another person to help out. If any Members of the Staff at either place were stressed, they certainly didn't show it. In fact, at Kat's especially, they seemed to thrive on being busy and boy, were they busy!

I have worked in establishments when we had more customers than we could handle. In fact, I was probably one of those people who looked stressed out. No more! Next time I find myself in that kind of situation, I will think of my two new role models, Maxine and Ashleigh, and I will do better. Because if they could perform that way, then so can I and so can most other people!

***Josh:***

Bravo Monica! Let me tell you about our final escapade. For me it was extraordinary. I will never forget it! Monica will introduce you to "Red".

***Monica:***

This Escapade began when Josh was having car trouble. Josh calls his car "Red". Something just wasn't right with Red, so Josh took him to a famous car shop because the Car was due for a tune up. They changed the oil and did some minor things which cost Josh $350.00, which turned out to be a major rip-off.

***Josh:***

I was so angry. After charging me $350.00 for doing practically nothing, this car shop told me they would like to check my car over because they thought something was wrong with the transmission. I didn't trust them. So, to make a long story short, I went to see someone I did trust to find out where the best Mechanic was. I went to see Max, yes Maxine from Summit Sporting Goods! You see, Max has a special love for cars too. Talking about cars with Maxine, was one of the reasons I had fun when I was trying on all those running shoes.

As it turned out, Max was on her day off, however, a fellow Sales- person and Co-Manager, Madeleine, told me she and all the members of her family always bring their car to the same place as Max does, Matthew's Garage. Madeleine also said that neither she nor Max would ever bring their cars anywhere else. I had found a loose fan belt, which the other place either didn't see or didn't bother to fix. But I knew something else was wrong with Red. So, off we went, both Monica and I, to Matthew's Garage. We didn't make an appointment, something we should have done. Things were so hectic with my Son having had an accident at school, my own school work , my concerns about Red and so on, that I just did not think to call. Realizing this on our way there, I kept wondering if I should stop and call this Fellow. However, with Red driving so poorly, I felt it was best to keep going. I just prayed that Matthew would help us out.

# CHAPTER 36

## The Power of Service
## The Presentation--THE FINALE

*(Monica had a soundtrack ready to go on her computer as Josh prepared to Rap.)*

**Josh:**

*Now listen everybody while I tell you a story,*
*About a very kind guy who was seekin' no glory,*
*His name is Matthew—he's amazing' & real*
*Like my Grandmother's Table, he is the real deal.*

*Matthew loved my Car--he made such a fuss,*
*It was mind-blowin' too how well he treated us;*
*If there were more Matthews in the world today,*
*We wouldn't have to rap about Service this way.*

*(Loud applause and encouraging cheers and whistles followed.)*

**Josh:**

Thank you all! We weren't sure how that would go over. We wrote it because Matthew did blow us away with both his Service and his Hospitality. We just showed up. He just dropped what he was doing and spent at least an hour with us. That was the first thing that impressed us, although I should also mention that the driveway into his place was beautifully lined with trees all along the fencing. It was a very appealing and welcoming entrance, totally unexpected for a place that fixes cars.

Right from the start, Matthew made us feel at home. It was obvious that he really cared about finding out what was wrong with my Car, my 'Bella Tesoro' as he called it, meaning 'Beautiful Treasure'. It wasn't just another car to him. He instinctively knew what Red meant to me.

However, that is not what I thought at first. No, at first I figured it was too good to be true. I mistook his sincerity for a sales pitch. I doubted his sincerity because I had never come across it before, not from a mechanic. It took a while before I realized that it was no act, that he was not feigning his enthusiasm, nor was he trying to impress me. He was just the real deal, as authentic and rare as my Grandmother Maya's extraordinary table.

More than anything else, Matthew made me feel important because I owned a car like Red. I definitely didn't feel that way at the other car shop--far from it! The truth is, who doesn't want to feel important? I mean that is what Service and Hospitality are supposed to do, right? You're supposed to feel like you matter. Otherwise, what's the point of service?

I'd be remiss if I didn't share with you how Matthew made me feel that way. Actually, If it were not for Monica, I would have left feeling fantastic but never really knowing why. Monica made me think about the whole experience by asking me important questions. She wouldn't let me off the hook either, until I answered those questions intelligently. That taught me why it's important to understand the special experiences we have in life, so we can emulate them.

***Monica:***

I pretty much observed and listened during the entire time that Josh and Matthew were talking. After some chat, Matthew led us to what he called 'his office', which was an outside picnic table. About half-way through our visit, he brought us tea and home-baked cookies from his house, if you can imagine that. He would not take no for an answer. His hospitality was both heart warming and highly unusual.

During our time at Matthew's 'office', AKA the picnic table, that is when Josh realized Matthew was for real. He asked Josh the right questions about his car, like a good doctor does when he is trying to come up with the correct diagnosis and just as Maxine had done. When Josh would respond, Matthew would ask more follow-up questions.

Once Josh explained it all to him, Matthew put the pieces together and concluded that aside from the loose fan belt, the wheel alignment and the alternator were causing Red's problems. It had nothing to do with the transmission which was mentioned by the first shop Josh visited, you know, the place that charged him $350.00 What if Josh had left his car at that shop?

Josh felt UNDERSTOOD because MATTHEW WAS REALLY LISTENING TO HIM, ASKING QUESTIONS AND TAKING NOTES. He was friendly but very serious during this discussion with Josh. It was evident that fixing up Red would cost a lot more than a pair of new running shoes and Matthew showed great sensitivity to the fact that Josh was a student in need of his help.

***Josh:***
Besides really listening and understanding what I was saying, it was evident that this Guy really knew his stuff. He was knowledgeable but not the least bit cocky or arrogant.

You could also see that Matthew was enjoying the whole process, like unravelling a dilemma and coming up with a solution.

There were no forms to fill out. The consultation was totally PERSONALIZED.

On looking back, Monica and I realized we actually had fun at Matthew's place. Have you ever had fun at a mechanic's garage when it involved your car? Sure, I was concerned about the cost. But who wouldn't be? The longer I was there, the more I wanted this Man and no one else to fix my vehicle.

The cost to fix my car? Well, it was not cheap but it was affordable and we definitely got full value. My beautiful red car now runs like a dream.

In addition to all that, Matthew made me feel appreciated and confident. My car has never run better. Matthew's initial diagnosis was exactly right.

I have never met a mechanic like Matthew or anyone else like him for that matter. I only wish all of there could have been invisibly present for that visit. It was something else!

Monica told me that Matthew left her with a sense of well-being because he always included both of us when he was talking. He always looked at both of us, just as Maxine made me feel included when she was serving Monica.

With our bad service experiences, we felt rushed. We did not feel rushed at any of our three great service experiences. If the Customer happens to be in a rush, that is their prerogative. Great service means being on the customer's time, right? However, we were in no rush during our visits, except when we picked up Red from Matthew's place. Then we were anxious to go for a drive. And you know, Matthew sensed that. He reacted quickly and we were on our way in no time.

So the prize for being most like my Gram Maya's Table goes to Matthew because he combined Service and Hospitality in a completely new way. He is a bona fide original, one of a kind! He turned getting your car fixed into an exceptional experience. That in itself is a miracle!

***Monica:***
Like Gram Maya's Table, there was something incredibly captivating and charismatic about Matthew. There's a kind of phenomenal energy that comes from that Table and that same kind of energy and enthusiasm was present in each of the stellar People we have told you about today. Hopefully, we have done them justice.

We also learned the huge importance of teamwork during this experience and that prize definitely goes to Kat's Seafood Paradise, not to mention the unforgettable phrase, 'We're on Your Time, not ours'.

If we were measuring Teamwork, then Kat's would win the prize. And Ashleigh, well she was an absolute delight as was the decors there. Summit Sporting Goods had a fun atmosphere and I felt a real rapport with Maxine. The only reason we did not choose Summit Sporting Goods is that we noticed a woman waiting a while to be served. However, in putting together Service and Hospitality, our choice for number one had to be Matthew. We're just wondering where his office is in winter!

You may have a different choice because Service is a very personal thing but one thing is for sure, Josh and I both have experienced the surprising power of service. Its power is so strong, it can make or break your day. Mediocre service can harm or even ruin the reputation of an entire business or institution. If retraining does not bring someone up to snuff, then they should either be relocated to another position or in some cases, they should be let go.

To be brutally honest, both Josh and I came to the following conclusion--that because of the great power of service, those whose only purpose is to receive a paycheque, are not worthy to attend to the needs of others.

YOU SEE, THE QUALITY OF SERVICE CAN ENRICH OR DIMINISH BOTH THE PERSON BEING SERVED AND THE PERSON PROVIDING SERVICE. ALTHOUGH THE PERSON BEING SERVED IS THE ONE PAYING, THE ONE PROVIDING THE SERVICE HOLDS THE POWER TO MAKE THAT PERSON FEEL GOOD, TO PRODUCE A NICE MEMORY, TO HAVE THE CLIENT AS A CONSTANT ADVERTISEMENT AND TO LEAVE THAT INDIVIDUAL FEELING BETTER THAN THEY DID BEFORE. IF THAT ISN'T POWER, THEN I DON'T KNOW WHAT IS!

Now for the question Josh and I have been seeking an answer to since we began this project. WHY DOES ONE BUSINESS HAVE

POOR SERVICE WHILE ANOTHER HAS OUTSTANDING SERVICE?

We do have an answer coming up but before we share it with you, it's sort of like asking, what is it about the Spaghetti Sauce at Restaurant X that makes it so much better than the Sauce at Restaurant Y? One person might say it's a special seasoning; another person might say it's something else, because it takes a multitude of ingredients to create an authentic, made from scratch spaghetti sauce. Likewise, it takes many different ingredients to achieve and deliver exceptional Service and Hospitality. That is what we have attempted to explain in our Story today—all the ingredients it takes to unleash the positive Power of Service.

At the Drug Store, at the Department of Tourism and at the second shoe store, there was a prevailing laziness in the air. Similarly, with the insurance company, where the recording fiasco spun Josh into outlandish and hopeless orbit. But at KAT'S PARADISE, at THE SPORTING GOODS STORE and at MATTHEW'S GARAGE, THERE WAS AN UNMISTAKABLE, POWERFUL ENERGY. THOSE PEOPLE WERE LIVELY AND ENGAGING. They had get-up-and-go; they were clued in and on the ball! IT WAS *A STATE OF MIND IN MOTION* AND IT WAS AS REAL AS I AM, STANDING HERE.

***LAZINESS HAS NO POWER OR PURPOSE. BUT ENERGY, ENERGY IS POWER. TO PUT IT ANOTHER WAY, MENTAL AND PHYSICAL ENERGY ARE THE GATEWAYS TO EXCEPTIONALISM!***

In conclusion, Our Service Escapades were, without a doubt, one of the most enlightening and life-changing experiences of our lives. I have grown up watching my Mother serve people in her own business, a gift shop. My Mother said to me, "You know Mia, very good service takes patience and a love for what you do, *even on those days when you don't love it so much.*"

I have often watched my Mother do just that in her business, on those days when she didn't love it so much and I have seen the power of service radiate from her, even restore her, on those days. When my Mother serves someone, she lights up and in the process lifts up others, as did Ashleigh, the Team at Kat's, Maxine and the inimitable Matthew. That is what I am going to work on. I want to be like them!

Thank you all. You have been a remarkable audience, and Josh, thank you so much!

***Josh:***

Monica, you have been a dream for a Partner and you are forever my mentor. For those who don't know this, Monica and I have been good friends since the ninth grade and believe me, she is the real deal.

There is one more person I want to thank, my Grandmother Maya. Without her magnificent Table, we may never have seen the light. My Grandmother also served people and in so doing, she improved her own life and enriched the lives of all those who knew her. Many of her Customers still talk about how special and wonderful she was. That is her legacy.

This whole experience has made me want to be a far better person. I have come to realize that service is also about how we treat the people we care about every day. I think we can serve them better too by making them feel great about themselves more often.

I never imagined I could learn so much from this Assignment. All I have to do now is put it all into practice.

Thanks so much for being such great Listeners! It's much more than we could have hoped for.

> *(The applause and cheers from the other students was deafening. Josh and Monica were obviously overwhelmed. Monica was trying her best to hold it together. They both felt relieved and surprised at the response from their classmates. But what did the Professor think?)*

***Professor Sydney:***

Ms. Flowers, Mr. Johnson, the loud applause from your Classmates is well deserved. May I say that your Presentation was much like your Grandmother's wonderful Table. Indeed that Table looks like a masterpiece. I think you two should collaborate and write a book about your 'Escapades' as you call them. You certainly brought them to life for all of us. I'd also like to add that your Presentation was pretty bare bones. You did not use PowerPoint or other aids. However, the power of your Presentation is undeniable. Few bells and whistles but a very substantial Presentation I must say. You walked the talk—it was energetic, authentic and meaningful. You obviously put in a great deal of time and work and it will serve you well, indeed. Congratulations to both of you.

Tori Desjardins raised her hand.

"Yes Tori, you have a question?" asked the Professor

"Yes, I think your Presentation was really great but it sounds as if it was all so easy for you. I mean some of us have very complicated lives and we don't have the time to go into such detail."

Josh took the question. "Yes, I understand exactly what you're saying Tori. But believe me, Monica and I had our share of unexpected events during this whole process. My Son was in the hospital; Monica was fired from a job for being late; we also moved plus we had the car trouble. So I can honestly tell you that it was not smooth sailing and not easy to find the time. I'd say it was more Monica's excellent insights and organizational skills that kept us on track."

"Sorry People," interrupted the Professor, "Our time is up. Please feel free to ask any further questions you may have for Mr. Johnson and Ms. Flowers at our next class. I hope you will think long and hard about their Presentation. There was a lot of meat in there and I intend to include some of the points they made in December's exam. Ms. Flowers, Mr. Johnson, are you able to stay behind or do you have another class now?" asked the Professor.

"No Sir, neither of us has a class now," replied Monica.

The Professor waited for the other students to leave the classroom.

# Chapter 37

## The Professor's Proposal

***"I want to put a ding in the universe."***

***Steve Jobs***

The Professor began: "You have both done a Grade A piece of work on this Assignment. The actual mark I will record for your Presentation is 95. You know it has been several years since I have given anyone over 90% on an assignment. Congratulations to both of you--Well-deserved indeed. I would like a copy of your Presentation—heaven only knows I have enough paper around here but nevertheless, I would like a copy. Oh and if you could include two five by seven inch photos of each of the Two Tables, that would be helpful. No rush, next week will be fine."

"Thank you Professor Sydney. We're honoured that you liked our Presentation," stated Monica.

"Yes, well it is obvious you two put in the work. You know, one gets very tired of these PowerPoint Presentations all the time. Oftentimes there is no power and no point. You put your hearts and souls into this. Anybody with half a brain can see that. Your Presentation was meat and bones, yes, with a good dose of seasoning."

Josh and Monica remained quietly respectful, as they hung onto every word the Professor uttered.

"I appreciated the way you explained the details of what made the great visits stand out. Your Ashleigh, Maxine and Matthew created their own brand of Service and Hospitality. They are Originals, one of a kind. Therein lies their exceptionality. And the Two Tables' idea, I don't mind saying, that was a stroke of genius. People won't forget it. I certainly will not forget it. I also like the fact that you included the power that a good letter can still have in today's digital world, the insurance company bit. I'm going to tell you something. You both have a talent for conveying a message. That is a type of power too you know. The word 'power' seems to have stayed with me," chuckled the Professor.

"Thank-you, Sir," replied Josh humbly, hardly believing his ears.

Both Monica and Josh maintained their composure. Inwardly they each felt a combination of relief and pure joy, neither realizing that the best news was yet to come.

The Professor continued: "I would like to make a proposal to both of you. Please hear me out. You see, I also teach a semester course, which is an abridged version of this one, for first year students. It begins in January and I like to use case studies for that course. In the summer I have various other projects and courses related to Service and Hospitality. I do have a Teaching Assistant but he is graduating and going back to his home. So, you see I have been keeping my eyes open for a couple of students who can take on some extra duties as TA's. I think that both of you would be very well-suited to such a position and by spreading the responsibilities between you, the extra load should not be overwhelming for you." Josh and Monica were listening and conveying their understanding through nods and supportive facial expressions. The truth was, they were both stoked to the hilt.

"So, I am wondering if either or both of you, hopefully both of you, would be interested in such a position? I think you would both make excellent Teaching Assistants. You have a strong presence, are both effective communicators and when you speak, you have a certain cogency which is critical to this kind of thing, although Mr. Johnson, I'm not sure about the rap thing," chuckled the Professor again. "Also you have shown that you can get things done thoroughly and with excellence. That alone is significant. What do you think? Would you be interested? If you are, I could fill you in on the details at my office next week. Ms. Flowers, you said at the end of your Presentation that you would like to serve people. You echoed that sentiment Mr. Johnson. Well, here is your chance."

Josh and Monica glanced at each other. They both knew their answer.

"Yes, Professor, I am certainly interested and flattered Sir. I would very much like to be one of your Teaching Assistants." responded Josh, extending his arm for a handshake. The Professor returned the handshake and was obviously pleased.

"How could I possibly refuse an offer like that Sir! Thank you for this opportunity. It is a wonderful and welcome surprise," declared Monica, as she too extended her arm to signal her acceptance of the Professor's offer.

"Ms. Flowers, people make their own opportunities. The pleasure is all mine, believe me. Your joint portrayal of the people who served you was very rich. You brought those people to life. And that is what an understanding of Service excellence requires. It's not easy being a TA, you know. Some students have the audacity to make up stories of visits that never took place. Others approach it as if it were a high school assignment. There were very few in the Class that were up to par. Yours was, to use your words, authentic and powerful. It was by far the best to be perfectly honest. Now don't let that go to your heads because I expect the same calibre of work from you in the future."

"I think I can speak for both of us, Sir, when I say that you can depend on us to do just that," affirmed Josh. "Monica and I tend to be hard on ourselves."

"Very good then. I'd like you to drop by my office next week so I can go over the details with you. Oh and do remember to give me a copy of your Presentation. Yes, you two should write a book one day, indeed. Well then, bravo and thank you for making my day with that Presentation of yours."

The Twosome graciously thanked the Professor, confirming that they would see him the following week with a copy of their Presentation and photos of the Two Tables.

Once Josh and Monica were out of earshot distance from the classroom, they simultaneously grabbed each other's hand and ran to the soft drink machine. Then, feeling drained and speechless, they quickly walked outside, took a long gulp of their drinks and searched for an unoccupied bench

"I don't believe what just happened!"

"Man, it's incredible. I never imagined that kind of reception or outcome. Monica, we are going to celebrate tonight! I'm going to cook you a fabulous dinner. And I have a little surprise for you. We can talk about all of this tonight and over the next few days but for now, let's just take it all in and bask in the success of our Presentation. And becoming a TA—can you imagine? I've never felt like this before." Josh then noticed that Monica was losing energy.

"Look, I've arranged for Mau to take Bean for the night so we can have a quiet dinner together. You've been up since 4am so you should get some rest."

"Sounds perfect," replied Monica. "Thanks JJ. Hey, we got 95, like the Barolo! And we both have TA positions. It's surreal."

"We'll celebrate over dinner but right now, I have to go and get us some groceries so we actually have a dinner and I want you to have a rest.

"Thanks JJ...for everything. It was such a blast working on this project—no, that's not the right word. There are no words for the way I feel right now. I just feel grateful and in a state of disbelief."

"You did fantastic Monica. I'm genuinely and authentically so proud of us. You made this happen. You pushed me. At least I had the good sense to listen to you. So now I'm going to take you home and you're going to rest. I'll wake you up in plenty of time to get freshened up."

Monica napped until they reached home. Josh felt a surge of energy as he was driving. He gently awakened Monica. "Meet you at Gram Maya's table, 8pm. You'd better be hungry!"

"Hey Josh," called out Monica. "Did you ever buy a gift for Maureen?"

"Yup. I bought her a musical treasure box, at your Mom's Shop. It's beautiful."

" What a great idea. See you at dinner, Maestro Cucinare...it means 'Grand Chef'."

Josh smiled. "Hopefully I'll earn that title tonight. Make sure you rest Monns, really."

"I will, I promise. Thanks Josh. We did good—woohoo!"

Monica dropped her coat in her room. She stretched out on her bed, still feeling high from all that had just happened. After ten to fifteen minutes, her eyes began to close involuntarily. For the first time in many weeks, she felt completely relaxed as she fell asleep.

# Epilogue

***"I've missed more than 9,000 shots in my career. I've lost almost 300 games. Twenty-six times I've been trusted to take the game-winning shot and missed. I've failed over and over and over again in my life. And that is why I succeed."***

***Michael Jordan***

When Monica awoke around 6:20pm, she could hear Josh working in the kitchen. She showered, put on a little makeup, fixed her hair and slipped into her favourite evening dress, the red one, which she had worn for their first Escapade. If Josh was going to all this trouble, she wanted to show him how much she appreciated it. Plus she felt that the vibrant red was a happy colour, just right for their celebration. She presumed that it was Josh's favourite colour too.

Monica felt rested and excited to talk over their day with Josh. She was jubilant and danced her way from the washroom to her bedroom.

"Hey Josh, Do you need any help?" With one arm through her dress and the other holding her makeup bag, Monica hoped that Josh's answer would be no. Plus she had a few decisions to make.

"No, just stay there and relax. I'll let you know when it's ready," he called out. Monica was happy to hear that, since she was trying to choose which shoes to wear and was still fighting with her dress. It wasn't an easy dress to get into but once it was on, it felt great.

While dinner was simmering, Josh rushed to get changed.

He had already showered while Monica was napping. He changed his shirt and ran back to the kitchen and began to set the table--Gram Maya's table of course. He stirred the sauce one more time and then knocked on Monica's door...."Dinner will be ready in five minutes Sweety."

Monica came out in her slim-fitting dress. The style was incredibly flattering. Josh was wearing a crisp white shirt, open at the collar. Monica always commented on this shirt whenever he wore it.

"Monica, you look absolutely beautiful!"

"Thank you. You Sir, look handsome and dashing." Josh pulled out a chair for Monica. "Have a seat and feel free to nibble on the platter. I tried to get all the fruits and things you like."

"Wow, the platter looks so pretty, I don't want to mess it up. Everything looks so lovely, Josh."

Josh was more than pleased. "Libation coming up mia Bella."

Josh brought out two beautiful silver wine goblets that Monica had never seen before. They looked as if they had been freshly polished. It was then that she realized just how much effort Josh had put into planning and preparing this meal. She had seen the goblets at his parents' home.

"Wow, these goblets are gorgeous !"

Josh then showed Monica the bottle of wine to ensure it was to her satisfaction. She checked out the label and then looked again.

She was flabbergasted. It was the Elio Altare Barolo Brunate!

"Joshua! Where on earth did you find this? I cannot believe it. Oh my God...this is all so beautiful and amazing! You have to tell me how you got this wine. They can't have had it on the shelf. Where and how did you get it?

"I have my ways," Josh replied proudly, as he slowly poured a small amount of the precious wine into Monica's goblet for tasting.

Monica took a healthy sip and threw her head back in pure delight. She was ecstatic. "It's exquisite, unbelievable Josh!" Monica knew her wines.

She quickly held up her goblet to make a toast. "Josh, you opened your home to me. You are the most generous person I know. My wish for you is that all you have done for me boomerangs back to you a thousand fold."

"Thank you Sweety. You've done as much or more for me and for Bean. Hey, since the spaghetti sauce is still simmering, how about if we take this platter and the wine to the coffee table. Let's relax there for a while."

"This bottle must have cost you a fortune."

"Don't worry about that. So, what did you think of the Professor's proposal, the Teaching Assistant offer?"

"I was and still am in disbelief about it...I love the idea, and you?"

"I do as well." Josh paused for a moment. "Monica, there's something I'd like to share with you before we have dinner, and before we have too much wine. I need you to be comfortably sober."

Josh took out an envelope and gave it to Monica. Inside the envelope was a card with a picture of a bouquet of roses and a message in Josh's handwriting. Monica read it silently.

*Dearest Monica,*

*The Barolo Brunate is a symbol to show you that I would go to the ends of the earth to make you happy. This Project has shown me that together we are unbeatable! Since you have moved in, Life has been so much happier for Bean and for me. Bean loves you. He keeps asking me if you will one day be his Mom.*

*I can no longer hold in the truth. I LOVE you and want to serve you that love every day until the end of time.*

*There is only one woman for me and that woman is you. I can only hope that you feel the same way. I Love you Monica. I always have and always will.*

*Forever Yours*
*Josh*

Tears were forming in Monica's eyes and then they began to stream down her face. Her mascara was bleeding; she was speechless. Josh went over and sat beside her. "Is it too much?" he asked softly. "The last thing I wanted to do was upset you, especially on this special day. If you don't feel the same way, I understand."

"No, no, it's beautiful! It's the most wonderful thing anyone has ever written to me." Monica took a sip of wine and then looked up at Josh, her hand quivering as she laid her goblet on the table.

"I do feel the same way. I love you so much in so many ways, in all the right ways. But I'm so scared that we'll lose our friendship, if we become romantically involved. I couldn't bear that. Our friendship is so precious to me." Monica nervously took another sip of wine.

"Okay then, we won't be romantic. We'll just love each other with no romance whatsoever," uttered Josh, holding her hand. "Whatever way you want it Sweety; whatever makes you happy. I'm at your service M'lady." Josh was trying his hardest to lighten the mood. He couldn't bear the thought of upsetting or losing Monica.

"JJ, you're so funny. That's one of the things I love about you. Monica picked up Josh's card and read it again. "You're right you know. Together we are unbeatable. I really do love you.

The truth is, I've often thought about us being together. I think you're the most incredible, extraordinary man I've ever known and I definitely do not want anyone else to have you!"

"Well then, my Sweet, follow me. I'm going to serve you Josh's Superbly Special Spaghetti Sauce, with your favourite pasta of course. And don't worry about our friendship; it will only grow stronger."

The Twosome had a marvellous time eating and chatting over dinner. They finished the bottle of wine, laughed and joked about how nervous they had been for their Presentation and recalled some of the funny and awkward moments they had faced during their Escapades. They relived several of the special moments of the last few months and found endless reasons to make toast after toast. They shared their feelings about how good it felt to be cheered and applauded so vigorously by their classmates, the impact of the Professor's gracious comments about their Presentation and the unexpected opportunity he was giving them. They were both humbled and electrified by his offer.

"I have a special dessert baked by The Pastry Shop and I made some coffee or I can brew up some tea if you like?"

"Coffee is just fine Josh. It's just all so exciting and dreamlike. I want to take in every moment, every single second!" Here, let me help you with that; then I have something to tell you, about what you said before. I've been thinking; who better to have as that one special person than your Best Friend?" Monica's thoughts were all running together. "And I love the idea of becoming a TA. That's a form of service too. You know, answering questions for students, encouraging them when things get tough, marking their papers, helping them to improve....I want to be the best TA possible!"

"You will be, Sweety. It's who you are. You'll make those students feel like they really matter because you believe they do matter. I'm feeling more comfortable by the minute about becoming a TA myself."

"Comfortable? Josh, you're going to be a fantastic TA! Your personality, your insight—you know you're going to be great. What am I going to do with you?"

Monica then embraced Josh passionately, placing her lips firmly on his. They kissed each other lovingly for several minutes. Josh broke the silence. "Wait until you see what I have planned for our next quest," he whispered flirtatiously. The Duo then relaxed on the sofa, cuddled together, each with a look of complete contentment.

As Monica dozed off, Josh made his way to his Gram Maya's Table. He felt that her spirit had given him the courage to be genuine and authentic that evening. Josh felt an inexplicable connection to The Table. "You're real and powerful, just like your former Owner," he whispered. "Life is good Gram. Thank you."